YORK HANDBOOKS

GENERAL EDITOR:
Professor A.N. Jeffares
(*University of Stirling*)

D0278146

ENGLISH GRAMMAR

Loreto Todd

MA (BELFAST) MA PH D (LEEDS)
Senior Lecturer in English,
University of Leeds

LONGMAN
YORK PRESS

YORK PRESS
Immeuble Esseily, Place Riad Solh, Beirut.

LONGMAN GROUP UK LIMITED
Longman House,
Burnt Mill,
Harlow,
Essex.

First published 1985
Second impression 1986

ISBN 0-582-79267-3

Produced by Longman Group (FE) Ltd
Printed in Hong Kong

Contents

Introduction

The uniqueness of each language

Languages are like people: they have much in common and yet they are subtly or sharply differentiated. One very simple illustration will clarify this point. All languages can express possession, as can be seen in the following table:

	A	B
English:	my boat	John's boat
French:	mon bateau	le bateau de Jean
Irish:	mo bhád	bád Sheáin

The resemblance is very apparent in column 'A' but much less so in 'B'. Our simple illustration from three related languages should help to make us aware that each language is unique in the way it patterns. Each language must therefore be described in terms of its unique patterning.

Language and medium

Just as we often equate 'literature' with a 'written literature', forgetting that oral literature preceded anything written, partly conditioned it and is still the chief means of literary expression throughout the world, we often equate 'language' and 'speech'. For most people this equation is no more harmful than the useful fallacy that the sun rises in the east and sets in the west. For those of us who wish to understand language more completely, however, it is necessary to avoid misconceptions. A language can be realised in both speech and writing. Speech is the primary medium in the sense that we all learn to speak before we learn to write; and we all speak a great deal more than we write. Although speech and writing influence each other, the rules associated with them are not identical. Speech is spontaneous, often casual and imprecise. There is no need for speech to be absolutely precise because the speaker can see if the listener understands and can rephrase an utterance if he does not. With writing, however, precision and clarity are essential because the writer must predict and solve the reader's problems in advance. The rules of grammar are based on the rules governing writing. An understanding of these rules will help us to read and write efficiently and accurately.

Uses of English

English is now the most widely used *lingua franca* in the world, being employed daily by over six hundred million people. For some, it is a mother tongue; for others it is the language of education, politics or commerce. For all, it is a flexible tool capable of expressing the needs and aspirations of its many users.

The grammar of English

A grammar of a language is an attempt to describe systematically what a native speaker intuitively knows. It is a listing of the rules of a language so that we may speak and write it with clarity and precision and hear and read it with understanding. Our grammar of English will describe words and the ways in which words interact and combine to form acceptable sentences.

Note: A small box □ preceding a word, phrase or sentence means that the usage is unacceptable.

Part 1

Definition of terms

IN EVERY SERIOUS APPROACH to the study of grammar, two basic assumptions are made. The first is that normal language material displays formal similarities and differences:

$$\begin{bmatrix} \text{I} \\ \text{I} \\ \text{I} \\ \text{I} \end{bmatrix}$$
got up this morning (at) 7 $\begin{bmatrix} \text{o'clock} \end{bmatrix}$.
made $\begin{bmatrix} \text{my} \end{bmatrix}$ bed.
cook<u>ed</u> $\begin{bmatrix} \text{my} \end{bmatrix}$ breakfast.
arriv<u>ed</u> (at) the office (at) 9 $\begin{bmatrix} \text{o'clock} \end{bmatrix}$.

The second is that similarities and differences of meaning are carried by similarities and differences in form.

Our task is to find the significance of the perceived similarities and differences and to express this significance in a consistent, economical manner.

The word 'grammar' has been defined in many ways, partly because languages are different and need to be described in terms of their individual characteristics, and partly because fashions change. All definitions of grammar have, however, one common denominator: they all deal with the ways in which sentences are constructed out of smaller units.

Levels of language

Spoken English can be thought of in terms of four levels:

Level 1: Sounds

The study of sounds and the way they pattern is called *phonology*. Every language has its own distinct inventory of vowels and consonants. In one variety of English, often referred to as B.B.C. English or R.P. (Received Pronunciation), there are twenty vowels and twenty-four consonants. There are many rules governing their combination. English, for example, can have three consonants occurring in a cluster as in:

splash

string

scratch

Notice, however, that there is a fixed order here:

Position 1	*Position 2*	*Position 3*
	p	l
s	t	
	k(c)	r

So, 's' must always come first in the cluster and either 'l' or 'r' in the third position. Other languages have different systems. Many African languages, for example, allow the cluster 'mb' to occur at the beginning of a word, as in:

mboma (python)   mbombo (namesake)

Such a combination is not possible at the beginning of a word in English.

In the written language, letters are rough equivalents of sounds. Some languages, like Spanish, show a good approximation between sounds and letters. Other languages, like English, show a very tenuous link between sound and letter, as becomes clear if we look at a few examples. The 'g' in 'garden' is different from the 'g' in 'gentle' although the 'g' in 'gentle' is pronounced the same as the 'j' in 'jelly'; 't' in 'talk' is very different from the 't' in 'motion' which is itself similar to the 's' in 'sugar' but not the 's' in 'saint'. Most peculiar of all, perhaps, are the words ending in 'ough', in that:

bough	*rhymes with*	cow
cough		off
dough		go
rough		stuff
through		new
thorough		kookaburra

It is because of this lack of agreement between sounds and letters in English that many people, including George Bernard Shaw, have tried to reform our spelling system. Shaw illustrated the absurdity of some English spelling conventions by showing that 'ghoti' could spell 'fish' if we take the 'gh' sound from 'enough', the 'o' sound from 'women' and the 'ti' sound from 'nation'.

The study of sounds (phonology) and the study of letters (spelling systems) are extremely interesting but will not be discussed further in this Handbook.

Level 2: Word forms
The words in most languages change depending on such factors as plurality:

boy   boys

and tense:

    sing   sang

The study of variation in words is called *morphology* and it includes such changes as those illustrated above as well as techniques of word building, such as:

    man

    man + ly = manly

un + man + ly = unmanly

Of the three syllables in 'unmanly', only 'man' can occur in isolation, so many linguists refer to it as a 'free morpheme'. The other two syllables are known as 'bound morphemes', that is, they are not free to occur on their own. Other examples of bound morphemes are 'dis' in 'disappear' and 'ise' in 'hospitalise'.

We shall study further aspects of morphology in the course of this Handbook.

Level 3: Word combinations

The order in which words occur has a marked effect on meaning as is clear if we examine the following:

a Venetian blind	Post the guard.
a blind Venetian	Guard the post.
Mary loves John.	a light blue
John loves Mary.	a blue light

The study of the way words combine and interact is called *syntax*. This level is fully explored in our Handbook.

Level 4: Meaning

Many words in English have several meanings. A 'key', for example, can refer to:

    a metal object with which we open a door

    a system of musical notes

    a black or white note on a piano

    a solution to a problem

In addition, many words change their meaning depending on the words with which they combine. Thus, in isolation, 'heavy' might be defined as 'not light' but it does not have such a meaning in:

    a heavy cold (that is, a very bad cold)

    a heavy smoker (that is, one who smokes a lot)

or:

    heavy dew (that is, thick dew)

The study of meaning is called *semantics* and, although it is a fascinating part of language, it will not be examined further here.

The following diagram offers a résumé of the above:

```
                        Language
                      /          \
              Speech            Writing
                 |                 |
Level 1        Sounds            Letters
                    \           /
Level 2            Morphology
                        |
Level 3              Syntax
                        |
Level 4            Semantics
```

We shall concentrate on Levels 2 and 3, studying the form and the functions of words and the ways in which words combine to form acceptable sentences.

Part 2

Word classes

LINGUISTIC DEFINITIONS are never easy because we are trying to use language to define language. It should not surprise us therefore to learn that it is not a simple matter to say what a word is. Some linguists have claimed that a word can occur on its own. This is true, but the word 'the' rarely, if ever, occurs on its own and yet we would want to call it a word. Other linguists have claimed that a word has one unit of meaning but we could argue that the italicised elements in the sentences

The train *stopped.*

The train *came to a standstill.*

involve the same meaning. In addition, if we look at the words 'cow' and 'bull' we can say that both words refer to animals, to bovines and to adults. Thus, they seem to share at least three units of meaning. Since we are dealing with the written language, we can avoid such problems and state that a word is a group of letters with a space on either side of it.

In English, many words can function in different ways. We can, for example, have:

Light the fire, please.

Put on the light, please.

I wore a light coat.

where 'light' can be a verb, a noun and an adjective. It is important, therefore, to see how a word is used in a specific context before we try to classify it. Keeping this in mind, however, we can still isolate nine word classes or parts of speech in English – namely, nouns, pronouns, determiners, adjectives, verbs, adverbs, prepositions, conjunctions and exclamations. Each of these word classes will be examined fully in subsequent chapters so, here, we will simply indicate the main properties of each word class.

1. Nouns

A noun has often been defined as the name of a person, animal, place, concept or thing. Thus 'John', 'lion', 'Leeds', 'beauty' and 'stone' are nouns. If one wishes to test an item, to see if it is a noun, one can use such test frames as:

(The) —— seemed very nice.
Her —— is precious.
ancient ——.

2. Pronouns

A pronoun, as the name suggests, is like a noun in that a pronoun can replace a noun or a noun phrase. Thus, in the sentence:

John presented *his book of verse* to *his mother.*

we can replace the sections in italics thus:

He presented it to her.

There is an almost infinite number of nouns in English but pronouns can be exhaustively listed. We do this in Part 4.

3. Determiners

Determiners also belong to a finite set. They are words like 'the' and 'a' and 'some', as in:

the tree   *a* big tree   *some* big trees

Determiners are a class of words which precede nouns or adjectives + nouns.

4. Adjectives

Adjectives are descriptive words that qualify and describe nouns, as in:

a *pretty* girl   an *excellent* meal

Adjectives can fill such frames as:

(The) —— $\left\{ \begin{array}{l} \text{sheep} \\ \text{mutton} \\ \text{dogs} \end{array} \right\}$ seemed very ——.

5. Verbs

Verbs are often described as 'doing words', words that express actions, processes or states:

John *fell.*   John *turned* green.   John *resembles* his grandfather.

Verbs fit into such frames as:

They ——.   We must ——.   It/he is ——ing.

6. Adverbs

Adverbs usually modify verbs:

John laughed *loudly.*

or modify adjectives:

John was *critically* ill.

and, on occasions, sentences:

I'll see you *tomorrow*.

Adverbs often end in 'ly'. A test frame for adverbs would be:

$$\text{He} \left\{ \begin{array}{l} \text{ran} \\ \text{spoke} \\ \text{tried} \end{array} \right\} \text{very} \underline{\quad}.$$

7. Prepositions

Prepositions are function words like 'at', 'by', 'for' and 'with'. They connect the noun or pronoun that follows them to some other unit or units in the sentence.

Leave your bag *at* the station.

He fell asleep *by* the river.

She paid a lot of money *for* it.

8. Conjunctions

Conjunctions are joining words like 'and', 'but', 'that', as in:

Jack *and* Jill.

I went in *but* I did not see him.

He said *that* he had finished with it.

9. Exclamations

Exclamations are also often called 'interjections'. The latter term tends to be restricted to monosyllabic outbursts such as:

Oh!   Ah!   Wow!

whereas the term 'exclamation' is often applied to a group of words such as:

Goodness gracious!   Heavens above!

We have now listed the main word classes in English. Some of these can be further subdivided but the above subdivisions are adequate for our description of English. One point should be stressed, however. Words in English are not rigidly fixed in any one class. We have already seen that 'light' can occur as a noun, a verb and an adjective. Similarly, a word like 'round' can be a preposition in:

The road took him round the bay.

a noun in:

It was his turn to buy a round of drinks.

a verb in:

It was dangerous to round the corner at such speed.

and an adverb in:

Let's have a look round.

Before deciding what part of speech a word is, we must always see how it functions in a particular sentence.

Exercises

1. Pick out all the nouns and pronouns from the following newspaper extract:

Believe it or not, a man called Weatherill has invented a contraption for mopping up waterlogged sportsfields. Equally incredible, the device is marketed by a Bob Frost and a Mr. Winter is the production manager.

All three men are singing in the rain as they soak up a flood of orders. They have already equipped thirteen county cricket clubs with 'Motomops'. According to the head groundsman at The Fenners (Cambridge), no cricket could have been played there without it this season.

2. Read the following sentences carefully and say which word class each item in italics belongs to:

(*a*) John ran *badly*.
(*b*) They have a *lovely* baby.
(*c*) He ran *round* the track.
(*d*) King Arthur *had* a *round* table.
(*e*) He *changed* his *mind*.
(*f*) *He* loves his garden.
(*g*) Give *her the* books.
(*h*) *Hey*! *What* do *you* think you're doing?
(*i*) It's a lovely *blue*.
(*j*) Come *with* me.

3. Pick out the adjectives and adverbs in the following passage:

He was a highly intelligent child. By the time he was five he could speak English and German fluently, could invariably do his arithmetic faster than his elder brother and was a good violinist. He was not perfect, however. He often threw stones at other children and he always cried when his mother told him he was naughty.

4. In the following sentences, words have been used in different functions. Study the sentences carefully and then say which part of speech the italicised word is in each case:

(*a*) The feathers on a duck's breast are called *down*.
(*b*) Get *down* at once.

(c) The rugby captain scored a *try*.
(d) He won't even *try* to sing.
(e) I have a *green* jumper.
(f) Which *green* do you prefer?
(g) I missed the *fast* train.
(h) I can't run *fast*.
(i) He neither ate nor drank during the *fast*.
(j) He pushed the wheelbarrow *round* the garden fence.
(k) How many *rounds* did the delivery-service make this week?
(l) I looked *round*.

Part 3

Beyond the word

IT IS CONVENIENT AT THIS STAGE to offer brief definitions of units larger than the word, although these too will be considered in greater detail later.

In English, sentences can be analysed in terms of three types of constituent, the word, the phrase and the clause. We have already introduced the word and will now turn our attention to the other units.

Phrases

Phrases are groups of words which form a unit and which do not contain a finite verb. Both parts of this definition require expansion. If we look at the phrase 'on the chair', we know that it can occur in such sentences as:

I put it on the chair.   I sat on the chair.

In both sentences, we can replace the phrase 'on the chair' by 'there':

I put it there.   I sat there.

Notice that we replace all three words by 'there' because a phrase is a unit. It has internal coherence. In addition, if I asked the questions:

Where did I put it?   Where did I sit?

the answer is likely to be:

On the chair

not □*on the* and not □*on chair*, but the entire phrase.

Secondly, we have said that a phrase does not contain a finite verb. Again, this is simple to illustrate. A finite verb form can be preceded by 'I', 'you', 'we', 'they'. Non-finite verb forms cannot. Thus, in English we can have:

I sing   I see

but not:

□I singing   □I seeing
□I sung   □I seen
□I to sing   □I to see.

We can say, therefore, that present participles such as 'singing', past participles such as 'sung' and infinitives such as 'to sing' are non-finite verb forms.

Clauses

Clauses are groups of words which contain a finite verb but which are not capable of occurring alone. If we examine the following sentences:

That is the place *where we met.*

When he came in he locked the door.

I'll do it *if you want me to.*

we realise that the italicised segments are similar to sentences but they could not occur in isolation.

Sentences

Sentences are groups of words, phrases or clauses that can occur in isolation:

That is the place.   He locked the door.   I'll do it.

In the written language, a sentence begins with a capital letter and ends with a full stop, a question mark or an exclamation mark.

There is a great deal more to be said about phrases, clauses and sentences, but these simplified definitions will serve our needs for the next few chapters.

Exercises

---

1. Pick out the phrases in the following sentences:

   (a) He dropped me at the station on the way to London.   (3 phrases)

   (b) The young man, singing loudly, walked into the busy street. (3 phrases)

   (c) At what time do you expect the London train?   (2 phrases)

   (d) He put all his prized possessions in a bag and buried it at the bottom of the garden.   (3 phrases)

   (e) To become a dancer was his greatest dream.   (2 phrases)

2. Underline all the clauses in the following passage, giving the finite verb in each clause:

   They did not know any of the people that they passed on the stairs on their way to their room. Their room, which was on the third floor, faced the sea. It was also possible, if you had good eyes, to see a little island in the distance. It was said that smugglers used to hide their contraband there. Nobody knew if that story was true although most of the locals believed it.

3. Punctuate the following passage. Then indicate the number of sentences and clauses in it.

   the tale implies that a bride must ask permission to use the resources she finds when she comes to live with her husband this principle is directly stated in the claim that is why my lord the bride does not get anything for herself if she wants anything she tells the people of the house what she needs and they get it for her

Part 4

Nouns, pronouns, determiners

IN PART 2, WE LOOKED BRIEFLY at word classes in English. We shall now examine these in considerably more detail.

Nouns

Number

In English, nouns can be either singular (that is, referring to one) or plural (that is, referring to more than one). The majority of nouns are regular and form their plural by adding 's':

ant	ants	cat	cats
boy	boys	dog	dogs

Nouns ending in a consonant + y form their plurals by changing 'y' into 'ies':

army	armies	city	cities
bully	bullies	lady	ladies

A few nouns which end in 'f' or 'fe' have 'ves' in the plural:

knife	knives	loaf	loaves
life	lives	wolf	wolves

Nouns ending in 'o', 's', 'sh', 'ss', 'tch' and 'x' tend to form their plurals by adding 'es':

potato	potatoes	glass	glasses
gas	gases	witch	witches
bush	bushes	fox	foxes

Some of the most frequently occurring nouns in the language form their plural by means of a vowel change:

foot	feet	mouse	mice
man	men	woman	women

A number of nouns have the same form in the singular and the plural:

deer	deer	sheep	sheep
fish	fish		

and some words adopted from other languages retain their original plurals:

formula	formulae/ formulas	kibbutz	kibbutzim
index	indices	phenomenon	phenomena

There are a number of nouns, like 'flock', which are singular in form but which refer to a number of persons, animals or things:

a committee   a shoal (of fish)

a herd (of cows)   a collection (of stamps).

These nouns occur with a singular form of the verb and are replaced by a singular pronoun:

The committee usually *meets* at 8 p.m. *It* will not, however, meet until 9 p.m. next week.

Gender

English nouns are either masculine:

boxer   bull   man

or feminine:

actress   mare   woman

or neuter:

book   flower   table

The term *gender* is applied to this subdivision of the noun. Animate beings, whether human or animal, are, depending on their sex, either masculine or feminine. Inanimate objects are neuter. Gender in English nouns becomes apparent when they are replaced by pronouns:

John is a good boy. *He* lives on a farm.

Mary is a good girl. *She* lives in the town.

The school is a good one. *It* attracts good students.

Notice, however, that plural nouns, whether animate or inanimate, are replaced by 'they':

The boys and the girls go home when *they* have finished school.

The schools are left empty when *they* are closed for the holidays.

One further point should be remembered. Often, in colloquial speech, cars, ships and countries are referred to as 'she':

My car is beautiful. *She* can do a hundred miles an hour.

Algeria is a rich country. *She* exports a great deal of oil.

When in doubt about which pronoun to use, always follow the simple rule: people take 'he', 'she' and 'they'; things take 'it' and 'they'.

Possession

English nouns only change their form when indicating plurality or possession. The indication of possession is often called the *genitive* or the *possessive* case. To form the possessive, we add an apostrophe plus 's' to the singular:

John's book   (that is, the book belongs to John)

the boy's book   (that is, the book belongs to the boy)

To form the possessive case of a plural noun, we add an apostrophe to regular plurals, and an apostrophe plus 's' to irregular plurals:

the boys' books   (that is, the books belong to the boys)

the children's toys   (that is, the toys belong to the children)

the men's houses   (that is, the houses belong to the men)

Singular nouns ending in 's' normally add an apostrophe plus 's' to form the possessive:

Charles's car   Keats's poetry

With regard to inanimate nouns, possession is usually indicated by the use of 'of', as in:

the leg of the chair

and not:

□the chair's leg

When 'of' is used to indicate possession, we do not need to use an apostrophe:

the many wives of Henry VIII   *or*   Henry VIII's many wives

Classes of nouns

Nouns in English can be classified in a variety of ways. First, we can subdivide them into *common* and *proper*. Nouns such as:

book   fly   tree

are called 'common' because these names represent all or any of the members of a group. Proper nouns refer to specific places:

Australia   Egypt

and specific people:

Abdul   Erica

In English, proper nouns (and the names of languages are proper nouns) are always written with an initial capital letter:

France	French	Pierre
Nigeria	Nigerian	Ayo
America	American	Ronald

Nouns may also be classified according to whether they are *concrete* or *abstract*. A concrete noun has a material existence:

flower   lamb   shepherd

An abstract noun, on the other hand, refers to ideas, concepts and qualities:

courage   duty   love

Perhaps the most essential classification of English nouns is whether or not they are *countable* or *uncountable*. ('Uncountable' nouns are also referred to as 'mass' nouns.) A countable noun is one that can occur in either a singular or a plural form and can, as its name suggests, be counted:

one book   two books   three books

An uncountable noun cannot occur in the plural and cannot be counted:

butter   furniture   mutton   snow

An important point to remember is that countable nouns in the singular can be preceded by 'a':

a book   a horse   a tree

whereas uncountable nouns are never preceded by 'a'. Thus, we say:

some butter   some snow

and not:

□a butter   □a snow

Pronouns

Pronouns belong to a closed set. That means we can list every pronoun that occurs in English. It is convenient to subdivide pronouns into eight different categories, namely (1) personal pronouns, (2) possessive pronouns, (3) reflexive pronouns, (4) demonstrative pronouns, (5) interrogative pronouns, (6) relative pronouns, (7) distributive pronouns and (8) indefinite pronouns.

We have already seen that some pronouns reflect gender, that is, 'he', 'she' and 'it'. Other pronouns reflect case. Three cases can be seen in English pronouns, the *nominative* which occurs as the subject of a sentence (see Part 8), the *possessive* which indicates possession and the *accusative* case which follows a preposition and which occurs as the object of a sentence (see Part 8):

Nominative: *I* have read the book.

                He has finished the meal.

                Who is singing?

Possessive: The teacher chose *mine*.

I'll take *yours* but not *hers*.

Theirs is the best.

Accusative: John took *me* for a walk.

Give that coat to *him*.

Mary saw *them*.

We shall now examine the eight types of pronoun.

1. Personal pronouns

These pronouns as well as reflecting number and case are also divided into first, second and third persons. The first person refers to the speaker or speakers.

I can swim.　　　*We* mustn't do that.

The second person refers to the person or persons being spoken to:

You should listen to your parents.

The third person refers neither to the speaker nor the hearer but to the person or thing (people or things) being discussed:

He is an excellent student.　　　*They* are very expensive.

The twelve personal pronouns are mainly used to replace nouns and noun phrases.

		Singular		*Plural*	
		Nom.	*Acc.*	*Nom.*	*Acc.*
1.		I	me	we	us
2.		you	you	you	you
3.	*masc.*	he	him		
	fem.	she	her	they	them
	neut.	it	it		

2. Possessive pronouns

There are seven possessive pronouns:

		Singular	*Plural*
1.		mine	ours
2.		yours	yours
3.	*masc.*	his	theirs
	fem.	hers	
	neut.	its	

Possessive pronouns do not take apostrophes.

3. Reflexive pronouns

There are eight reflexive pronouns:

		Singular	*Plural*
1.		myself	ourselves
2.		yourself	yourselves
3.	*masc.*	himself	
	fem.	herself	themselves
	neut.	itself	

Reflexive pronouns are used in two main contexts. They occur when the same person is the subject and the object of a verb:

I cut *myself* with a knife.

You'll kill *yourselves* if you work too hard.

It (that is, the candle) burned *itself* out.

Secondly, they can be used for emphasis:

The champion *himself* attended to me.

She *herself* has no money but her father is wealthy.

It is worth stressing the difference between 'themselves' and 'each other'. If we look at the sentences:

They loved themselves.   They loved each other.

The first sentence is a criticism. It implies that John loved John and Mary loved Mary. The second sentence, however, implies that John loved Mary and Mary loved John.

4. Demonstrative pronouns

The four demonstrative pronouns are used to indicate closeness to or remoteness from the speaker. 'This' and 'these' indicate items which are close to the speaker and 'that' and 'those' indicate items which are not close to the speaker in space or time:

This is a book.   *That* was a lie.

I'll take *these*.   *Those* were good times.

5. Interrogative pronouns

The five interrogative pronouns, 'what', 'which', 'who', 'whom' and 'whose' are used in asking questions:

What happened?   To *whom* did you speak?
Which did you hit?   *Whose* are these?
Who said that?

'Whom' is the only interrogative pronoun that is marked for case. It is accusative and is used after a preposition:

With whom did you go?

and as the object of the verb:

Whom did you see?

In colloquial English, 'whom' is rarely used and the two previous questions would normally appear as:

Who did you go with?   Who did you see?

6. Relative pronouns
These pronouns introduce clauses. They are 'that', 'which', 'who', 'whom' and 'whose', and they are used as follows:

I've just sat on the hat *that* I bought.

The letter *which* he sent me last week has still not arrived.

John was the man *who* reversed into the wall.

The people on *whom* we rely are very kind.

The boy *whose* father died has gone to live with his uncle.

7. Distributive pronouns
There are six of these in English, namely 'all', 'both', 'each', 'either', 'neither' and 'some'. Often, these pronouns are followed by phrases such as 'of you' or 'of them':

All (of you) will go.

Both (of you) should come.

Each (of them) will receive £100.

Either (of you) will do.

Neither (of them) can read or write properly.

Some (of you) will have to go.

8. Indefinite pronouns
These are the pronouns 'any', 'some' and the compound forms 'anything', 'anyone', 'something' and 'someone':

I don't want *any*.   Has *anyone* seen my brother?

Take *some*. I have too many.   *Someone* was hurt.

In certain contexts, 'so' and 'such' also act as indefinite pronouns:

I don't think *so*.   *Such* is the way of the world!

Determiners

Like pronouns, determiners belong to a closed set and so can be exhaustively listed. They function like adjectives in that they precede nouns. There are five common types of determiners: articles, demonstratives, possessives, numbers and indefinite determiners.

1. Articles

There are three articles in English, the definite article 'the' and the indefinite articles 'a' and 'an'. The form 'a' is used before consonants whereas 'an' is used before vowels or a silent 'h'. As the names imply, 'the' is used when we wish to imply that the noun is definite in being relatively unique:

the moon   the sun   the world

or in being known to the speaker and the hearer:

He was *the* man we met in the supermarket.

The indefinite articles are used when we are not specifying anyone or anything in particular:

an honest child   a carpenter   an ant   a banana

2. Demonstratives

There are four demonstrative determiners (sometimes called 'demonstrative adjectives'), 'this', 'these', 'that' and 'those', as in:

this pen   these pens   that book   those books

Students will notice that these four words can also occur as pronouns. The difference between their usage as pronouns and as determiners can be seen in the following sentences:

This is a book.   (pronoun)

This book is mine.   (determiner)

I'll have *these*.   (pronoun)

I'll have *these* bananas.   (determiner)

What is *that*?   (pronoun)

Who is *that* man?   (determiner)

Those aren't mine.   (pronoun)

Those books aren't mine.   (determiner)

Determiners are followed by nouns. Pronouns are not.

3. Possessives

There are seven possessive determiners (also referred to as 'possessive adjectives'). These are 'my', 'your', 'his', 'her', 'its', 'our' and 'their'. These forms do not change as between singular and plural:

| my book | my books | its feather | its feathers |
| my box | your boxes | their home | their homes |

4. Numbers
Numbers, both cardinal and ordinal, can occur as determiners:

one student   first degree

However, numbers are only determiners when they are followed by nouns:

five fingers   six soldiers

5. Indefinite determiners
There are a number of indefinite determiners in English, the most widely used of which are the following:

some	some money	few	few politicians
any	any problems	much	much industry
all	all students	more	more effort
enough	enough food	most	most employers
no	no happiness	fewer	fewer patients
both	both parents	less	less meat
each	each child	either	either hand
every	every citizen	neither	neither group

We have now looked at nouns, pronouns and determiners and seen that the same item can belong to more than one word class. It is worth repeating that, as far as English is concerned, we must always look at how a word functions in a particular utterance before we can assign it to a specific word class.

Exercises

1. Underline the nouns in the following passage. Indicate whether the noun is common or proper:

   Manchester United put up a magnificent display on Saturday to win the cup. The game was fast-moving and exciting. The pitch was dry, the spectators cheerful and the players energetic. The game had everything, entertainment, excitement and a tense finish.

2. Say whether each of the nouns in the following list is concrete or abstract:

| beauty | cat | leisure | loaf | wealth | worm |
| brick | courage | lettuce | love | wheel | worry |

3. Replace the nouns in italics by pronouns:

(*a*) *John* has two brothers.
(*b*) *The continents* are drifting farther apart.
(*c*) I saw *Mary* yesterday.
(*d*) *Books* are very expensive.
(*e*) That pen is *John's.*

4. Say whether the words in italics are pronouns or determiners. (Remember that determiners are followed by nouns.)

(*a*) What are *those*?
(*b*) *The* sky is very dark.
(*c*) *Some* children have *no* brothers or sisters.
(*d*) *That* is *my* book.
(*e*) It is not *yours.*
(*f*) I haven't *any* money.
(*g*) *We* live on *our* farm.
(*h*) *Every* child should go to school.
(*i*) I'd like *four* apples, please.
(*j*) Give *that* book to *me*.

5. In the following sentences, identify the determiners and classify them according to type – that is, say whether they are articles, demonstratives, possessives, numbers or indefinite determiners.

(*a*) The man will soon cut down his trees.
(*b*) This book will give her no pleasure.
(*c*) I was delighted to receive your letter.
(*d*) Six young men arrived in a bus.
(*e*) Few people can have heard the news.

Part 5

Adjectives, verbs, adverbs

Adjectives

Adjectives are words which describe nouns. They fit into such test frames as:

(The) —— $\left\{ \begin{array}{l} \text{girl} \\ \text{food} \\ \text{books} \end{array} \right\}$ seemed very ——.

Notice that adjectives can occur in two positions. When they occur before the noun as in:

a *good* girl   a *lovely* dream   *happy* children   *cross* dogs

they are called *attributive* adjectives. They can also occur after verbs like 'be', 'seem', 'become', 'grow':

The boy was *thin*.   The boy became *angry*.
The boy seemed *happy*.   They boy grew *tired*.

Adjectives which occur after verbs are called *predicative* adjectives.

Positive, comparative, superlative

Adjectives may occur in three forms, called *positive*, *comparative*, *superlative*:

Positive	Comparative	Superlative
big	bigger	biggest
fat	fatter	fattest

Their use is illustrated by such constructions as:

John is a big boy.
Peter is bigger than John.
George is the biggest.

Short, monosyllabic adjectives like 'long' and 'strong' form their comparatives and superlatives by adding 'er' and 'est':

long	longer	longest
strong	stronger	strongest

This rule also applies to commonly occurring disyllabic adjectives like 'clever', 'simple', 'stupid' and to those which end in 'y':

clever	cleverer	cleverest
lazy	lazier	laziest
lovely	lovelier	loveliest
simple	simpler	simplest

Less commonly occurring disyllabic adjectives like 'hateful' and all polysyllabic adjectives like 'objectionable' form their comparatives and superlatives by the use of 'more' and 'most':

beautiful	more beautiful	most beautiful
hateful	more hateful	most hateful
loathsome	more loathsome	most loathsome
objectionable	more objectionable	most objectionable
ridiculous	more ridiculous	most ridiculous

Irregular adjectives

Most adjectives in English are regular, but a few (and among them the most frequently used in the language) are irregular:

bad	worse	worst
far	farther	farthest
	further	furthest
good	better	best
old	older	oldest
	elder	eldest
well	better	best

Two adjectives 'far' and 'old' have two comparatives and superlatives. For most purposes, one can avoid 'farther' and 'farthest' in that they tend to be used only to indicate distance:

I went much farther than I had intended.

'Further' and 'furthest' can be used both with regard to distance:

He threw the ball further than I did.

and in metaphorical structures:

John claimed that 85 per cent of the dancers were under eighteen. I would go further and claim that 90 per cent were under sixteen.

When in doubt about usage, select 'further' and 'furthest'. As far as 'old' is concerned, the irregular forms 'elder' and 'eldest' are limited to family expressions such as:

the elder daughter

the eldest of all her children

For most purposes, 'older' and 'oldest' should be selected.

Spelling

When an adjective ends in a vowel plus one consonant, the consonant is doubled before 'er' and 'est':

big	bigger	biggest
fat	fatter	fattest

but this doubling does not occur when the adjective has two vowels:

clean	cleaner	cleanest
neat	neater	neatest

or ends in two consonants:

bold	bolder	boldest
vast	vaster	vastest

Word order

When adjectives co-occur, they do so in a fixed order. A few examples will illustrate this:

the pretty little green cottage

the ugly big grey wolf hound

the lovely big old tree house

When adjectives co-occur, descriptive adjectives like 'lovely', 'nice', 'pretty' usually precede adjectives of size such as 'big', 'large', 'little'; adjectives of size precede adjectives of age like 'old' and 'young' which, in turn, precede adjectives of colour such as 'black', 'blue' and 'green'; adjectives of colour generally precede any noun that is used adjectivally, as 'wolf' and 'tree' are in our examples. It is unusual to have more than three adjectives co-occurring and the following rule indicates the order in which they habitually occur:

(descriptive) + (size) + (age) + (colour) + (noun)

Verbs

In English, words which occur in the following frame are verbs:

He
It } may ——
You

Regular verbs can take the endings 's', 'ing' and 'ed':

looks	looking	looked

and even irregular verbs can take the 'ing' ending:

being	having	seeing	taking

A list of irregular verbs is provided in the Appendix.

It is useful to be able to refer separately to two different parts of the verb phrase. An example will illustrate this:

(He) might arrive.

'Arrive' is called a *headverb* and 'might' is called an *auxiliary verb* because it helps to make more precise the information carried by the verb.

The following terms comprehend the distinctions we wish to make with regard to the verb:

Label	Examples (Regular, Irregular)
base form (this is the form used when giving orders)	look, sing
past tense	looked, sang
non-past (present) tense	look/looks, sing/sings
infinitive	to look, to sing
present participle	looking, singing
past participle	looked, sung

The table above shows that there are two *tenses* in English, a past tense and a non-past tense:

I saw him yesterday.   (past tense)

I see him every day.   (non-past tense)

'Tense' is the term that describes temporal changes that are made in the verb. In English, temporal distinctions are often made by adverbs. In the sentence:

I went to school.

the form of the verb tells us that the action took place in the past. In such sentences as the following, however:

I go to school every day.   I go to France tomorrow.

there is no difference in the verb usage but the first sentence tells us that the action is performed regularly, whereas the second refers to the near future. Such information is provided by 'every day' and 'tomorrow'.

The past tense
For regular verbs in English, the past tense is formed by adding 'ed' or 'd' to the base form of the verb:

look   looked   wave   waved

The past tense form does not change according to either person or number:

I looked   we looked
he looked   they looked
you looked

The main uses of the past tense
(*a*) To refer to actions, states or events which took place before the moment of narration, that is, when we use the past tense, we exclude the present moment:

I *lived* here for a year.   (This implies that I no longer live here.)
I *waited* for an hour.   (This implies that I am not waiting now.)

(*b*) It is often used in dependent clauses to refer to a possibility or a hypothesis:

I wish I *knew* how to fly (but I don't).
I would welcome him if I *saw* him (but I probably won't).

(*c*) It is used in indirect speech. If, for example, a person using the non-past tense says:

'I *sing* in the choir.'

this will be reported as:

He said that he *sang* in the choir.

The non-past (present) tense
Traditionally, the tense in such sentences as:

I *love* my children.   I *walk* to school.

has been called the 'present tense', but modern scholars prefer the name 'non-past tense' because this tense is not limited to descriptions of present actions, events or states.

The non-past tense has two forms. The base form of the verb is used unchanged with first and second person pronouns and with all plural subjects:

I sing   they sing
you sing   the men sing
we sing

When the subject is either 'he/she/it' or a singular noun, the verb form is modified in that 's' or 'es' is added to the base form:

He/she *sings*.   It *catches* mice.
The young man *sings*.   He *watches* us all the time.

The main uses of the non-past tense
(*a*) To express eternal truths, proverbial wisdom, timeless realities:

Peace *has* its victories.

Many hands *make* light work.

Water boils at 100° centigrade.

(*b*) It occurs in spontaneous commentaries and is a marked feature of sports reporting:

Whiteside *kicks* the ball to Robson who *moves* it across to Stapleton. Stapleton *chips* it to Wilkins who *loses* it to Case.

(*c*) It is chosen for such formulaic utterances as:

I *name* this ship 'Invincible'.

I now *pronounce* you man and wife.

I *declare* this bridge open.

I *beg* your pardon.

I *dare* you to.

(*d*) It is also used in describing habitual occurrences:

He *travels* to school by bus.

They *make* their own clothes.

She *advises* customers on their rights.

The expression of future time
Although there is no future tense in English, reference to the future can be made in the following ways:

(*a*) will/shall + base form of the verb:

I shall go to London next week.

He will return from Paris tomorrow.

There is considerable uncertainty among native speakers of English regarding the use of 'will' and 'shall'. Many never use 'shall' at all; some only use 'shall' in very formal situations. In the written medium, it is perhaps best to follow the rule:

I/we + shall

you/he/she/it/they + will

In the spoken medium, the reduced form ''ll' will occur most frequently:

I'll come to see you when I can.

He'll never be able to carry all that.

You'll have to hurry if you want to catch your train.

(*b*) be going to + base form of the verb:

> I'm going to drive to London tomorrow.
> He is going to sail round the world.

(*c*) be + present participle:

> I'm flying to France next week.
> She's coming home as soon as she can.

(*d*) the simple non-past:

> I sit my final examination next week.
> He arrives tomorrow.

(*e*) will/shall + be + present participle:

> He will be flying from Heathrow.
> We shall be working for the next two weeks.

Aspect in English

As well as temporal distinctions which are made overt in the verb phrase, English also makes distinctions relating to the continuity or non-continuity of an action:

> I was walking home when we met.
> I walked home.

and the completion or non-completion of an action:

> I have read the book.   (that is, I have finished it)
> I read that book last night.   (that is, but I may not have finished it)

'Aspect' is the term applied to these distinctions.

In English, we have two types of aspect: the progressive/continuous aspect and the perfect aspect.

(*a*) *Progressive/continuous aspect*: This involves the use of 'be' + the present participle:

> I am singing.
> (that is, the activity is occurring now and is continuous)
> He was singing.
> (that is, at a particular moment in the past the action was occurring and was continuous)

(*b*) *Perfect aspect*: This usage implies that an action has been completed:

> I have painted the door.   (that is, the task is complete)
> He had painted the door.   (that is, at a specific time, the task was complete)

The table below shows the range of tense and aspect usage in English:

Label	Regular verb	Irregular verb
Simple past	he looked	he sang
Simple non-past	I look	I sing
	he looks	he sings
Past progressive	he was looking	he was singing
	we were looking	we were singing
Non-past progressive	he is looking	he is singing
	I am looking	I am singing
	we are looking	we are singing
Past perfect	he had looked	he had sung
Non-past perfect	he has looked	he has sung
	I have looked	I have sung
Past perfect progressive	he had been looking	he had been singing
Non-past perfect progressive	he has been looking	he has been singing
	I have been looking	I have been singing

Auxiliary verbs

We have seen that there are, in English, headverbs and auxiliaries. The auxiliaries have the following characteristics:

(*a*) They always precede the headverb:

I *am* singing.   *Has* he gone?   He *may* not come.

(*b*) At least one auxiliary is obligatory in questions and negatives:

Do you like cheese?   You *cannot/can't* say that.

Can you drive?   *Don't* do it.

(*c*) They are used in tag questions:

You can't sing, *can* you?   You might come, *might*n't you?

You don't like her, *do* you?   He ran fast, *did*n't he?

Notice that where an auxiliary occurs in the main sentence, the same auxiliary is used in the tag question. If no auxiliary is used in the main sentence, then a form of 'do' is used in the tag:

You love her, *do*n't you?   He drives badly, *does*n't he?

(*d*) They can be used for emphasis:

I *can* sing.   You *will* go.

This usage is most frequent when making an emphatic assertion or denial:

'You can't sing.'   'I <u>can</u> sing.'

'You like cheese.'   'I <u>do not</u> like cheese.'

(*e*) If more than one auxiliary verb is used, the main stress usually falls on the first auxiliary:

I *must* have met you before.

I *shall* have been living here for two years soon.

(*f*) Most auxiliaries have strong and weak forms, with the weak form being preferred in rapid speech. Below, we provide a list of the auxiliaries which have weak forms and we give their phonetic equivalents. Where a written equivalent of a weak form exists, that is also given.

	Auxiliary	*Strong form*	*Weak form*	*Written equivalent*
	can	/kæn/	/kən/	
	could	/kʊd/	/kəd/	
	must	/mʌst/	/məs/	
	shall	/ʃæl/	/ʃəl, əl/	'll
	should	/ʃʊd/	/ʃəd/	
	will	/wɪl/	/əl/	'll
	would	/wʊd/	/wəd, əd/	'd
HAVE	have	/hæv/	/həv, əv/	've
	has	/hæz/	/həz, əz/	's
	had	/hæd/	/həd, əd/	'd
BE	am	/æm/	/əm/	'm
	are	/ɑ:/	/ə(r)/	're
	is	/ɪz/	/əz, z/	's
	was	/wɒz/	/wəz/	
	were	/wɜ:/	/wə(r)/	

(*g*) All auxiliaries can be followed directly by 'not/n't':

I cannot/can't sing.   I haven't heard any news yet.

This characteristic is in contrast to headverbs which cannot be followed directly by 'not/n't':

▢I like not it.   ▢He maden't it.

The auxiliaries can be subdivided into four categories: modals, the perfective auxiliary 'have', auxiliary 'be' and the dummy auxiliary 'do'.

1. Modals

In English there are nine auxiliaries which, because of their grammatical behaviour and their meaning, are classified as *modals*. These verbs are:

can	may	must	shall	will
could	might		should	would

They are called 'modals' because they relate to the 'mood' or 'attitude' of the speaker in expressing views on:

ability:

I can swim now but I couldn't swim last year.

futurity:

I shall drive to the city tomorrow.

He said he would drive to the city the following day.

insistence:

You will go, whether you like it or not.

It was impossible to dissuade him. He would do it his way.

intention:

I shall visit you next October.

They will come when they can.

obligation:

I must go now. I have a train to catch.

We mustn't behave like the others. We must behave properly.

permission:

You may now leave the room.

I wonder if I might get my ball out of your garden, please.

possibility:

We may come. It all depends on how much free time we have.

He might manage it, but I'm very doubtful.

probability:

It is very likely that he will visit us.

I shall come unless something very unexpected happens.

willingness:

I shall certainly come if I can.

I should love to visit you.

All modals are followed by the base form of the verb:

I can/could/may/might *go.*

This fact distinguishes modals from a number of near synonyms:

can = be able

but 'can' takes the base form of the verb, whereas 'be able' takes the infinitive:

I can *drive.*   I am able *to drive.*

must = ought

I must *work* harder.   I ought *to work* harder.

2. Perfective auxiliary 'have'

'Have' can be either a headverb or an auxiliary, a fact that becomes clear when we examine such sentences as:

My father has two wives.   My father has been to Beirut.

I have a beautiful car.   I have always told the truth.

In the first two sentences 'have' is used as a headverb and has the meaning of 'possess', whereas in the third and fourth sentences 'have' is used as an auxiliary modifying the meaning of the headverbs 'be' and 'tell'. When 'have' is used as an auxiliary, it is followed by the past participle of the verb it modifies:

I have seen the pyramids.   He has swum the channel.

3. Auxiliary 'be'

'Be' has many roles in English. It is a full headverb in such sentences as:

I am a student.   She was a doctor.

You are an examiner.   They were fortunate.

He is a teacher.

As an auxiliary verb, 'be' can perform two functions. When it is followed by the present participle of the verb it modifies, it is called the 'progressive' or 'continuative' auxiliary and it is used to express progressive aspect:

I am singing.   He was fighting.

When it is followed by the past participle of the verb it modifies, it is called the 'passive' auxiliary:

I was hit by a cricket ball.   He was never seen again.

When the subject of a sentence is the agent of the action, as in:

I hit John.   John threw the ball.

we say that the sentence is in the 'active voice' or, more simply, *active.*

When the subject receives the action, as in:

John was hit (by me).   The ball was thrown (by John).

we say that the sentence is in the 'passive voice' or is *passive*. Notice that in passive sentences in English we have the option of giving or omitting the agent, that is, we can say either:

The ball was thrown by John.

or

The ball was thrown.

These sentences are both passives but the second one is known as a 'truncated' passive because it does not provide all available information. We often use truncated passives to avoid laying blame or responsibility:

He was hit.   The match was lost.

4. Dummy auxiliary 'do'

Modern English needs an auxiliary verb to form both negatives and interrogatives. Whereas Shakespeare could write:

I like it not.   Like you that?

we must use:

I do not like it.   Do you like that?

When no other auxiliary occurs with which to form the negative or the interrogative, 'do' is used. It is called the *dummy auxiliary* because although it is grammatically very significant, its meaning is negligible. In a question like:

Can you swim?

the auxiliary asks for information on the listener's ability, whereas in:

Do you swim?

the auxiliary is merely used to form a question.

Summarising the above information on auxiliaries, we can offer the following table:

Auxiliary	Example
Modal	I must go now.
Perfective	I have finished this book.
Continuative	I am going home.
Passive	I was followed home.
Dummy	Did you hear the news?

These auxiliaries may occur together but only in a fixed order which can be written as:

(Modal) + (Perfective) + (Continuative) + (Passive) + Headverb

as in:

He must train.
He must have trained.
He must have been training.
He must have been being trained.

It is rare, however, to have four auxiliaries occurring together in such a way.

Adverbs

These words can modify verbs:

She sang *loudly*.

sentences:

Certainly, we shall win the match.

adjectives:

She was *exceptionally* beautiful.

and other adverbs:

She sang *very loudly*.

Many adverbs are related to adjectives:

Adjective	*Adverb*
careful	carefully
loud	loudly
quiet	quietly
rude	rudely

Like adjectives too, adverbs can have comparative and superlative forms. A few very common adverbs form their comparatives and superlatives by adding 'er' and 'est':

early	earlier	earliest
fast	faster	fastest

but most adverbs form their comparatives with 'more' and their superlatives with 'most':

angrily	more angrily	most angrily
often	more often	most often
quickly	more quickly	most quickly

There are a few irregular adverbs, the most frequently used of which are:

badly	worse	worst
far	farther	farthest
	further	furthest
little	less	least
much	more	most
well	better	best

The commonest types of adverb

(a) *Adverbs of time*: These tell us when an action or event occurred. Our list is illustrative rather than exhaustive:

now	frequently	soon	tomorrow
often	seldom	today	yesterday

(b) *Adverbs of place*: These tell us where an action or event occurred:

here	near	everywhere
there	yonder	nowhere

(c) *Adverbs of reason*: These tell us why an action or event occurred:

because	so (as)	since
for	so (that)	

(d) *Adverbs of manner*: These tell us how an action or event is performed:

angrily	beautifully	carefully	foolishly
well	precisely	nobly	ably

(e) *Adverbs of comparison*: Pairs of adverbs are involved in comparisons:

as . . . as	He is *as* good *as* gold.
less . . . than	He has *less* money *than* his brother.
more . . . than	He is certainly *more* willing *than* he used to be.

(f) *Adverbs of contrast*: The main items here are:

although	He won the match *although* he played badly.
despite	*Despite* his appearance, he is a man of wealth.
(even) though	I like him even *though* I know he doesn't like me.

(*g*) *Adverbs of condition*: The three main ones are:

if	*If* he is not here soon, I'll go without him.
unless	They will not do well *unless* they work harder.
whether . . . (or not)	I'm starting at 5 p.m. *whether* he's here *or not*.

(*h*) *Adverb question words*: The following question words are adverbs:

how?　　　　when?　　　　where?　　　　why?

(*i*) *Intensifiers*: A number of adverbs intensify the meaning of adjectives and adverbs. Two of them:

too/far too　　　very

can only occur pre-adjectively or pre-adverbially:

| He drives (*far*) *too* fast. | He sings *very* badly. |
| She is *too* thin. | She is *very* tall. |

Others, such as:

awfully　　　extremely　　　frightfully　　　terribly

can occur in the same slot as 'too' and 'very':

He drives *awfully* badly.　　　She is *extremely* thin.

They can also modify a verb:

My foot hurts *awfully/terribly*. I liked her *extremely*.

Students should avoid this second use of 'awfully', 'extremely' and 'frightfully' and select an adverb that is more appropriate to the context. These adverbs, like the adjective 'nice', are so frequently used in certain speech contexts that they have lost most of their original meaning and force.

Differences between adjectives and adverbs

Often, the same word can function as both an adjective and an adverb:

He owns a *fast* car.	(adjective)
He drives too *fast*.	(adverb)
The bread was *hard*.	(adjective)
He hit me *hard*.	(adverb)

In the first and third sentences, the words 'fast' and 'hard' give us information about the nouns 'car' and 'bread' and so they are adjectives. In the second and fourth sentences, they tell us something about the way he 'drives' and 'hits' and so we are dealing with adverbs. In isolation, it is not always possible to say what part of speech a word is, but when we examine the way a word functions in the particular context, its class becomes more apparent. It is therefore necessary to examine each word in context before trying to classify it. The following generalisations will, however, assist in the task of distinguishing between adjectives and adverbs.

ADJECTIVES are used in two main ways:

(*a*) before nouns:

    a *lovely* girl   *friendly* people   the *happy* man

(*b*) after verbs like 'be', 'become', 'grow', 'seem':

    She is *lovely*.   They grew *weary*.

    He became *angry*.   The men seemed *happy*.

ADVERBS are used in four main ways:

(*a*) to modify verbs:

    He drove *furiously*.   She ran home *quickly*.

(*b*) as intensifiers:

    I'm *very* angry.   He sang *terribly* badly.

(*c*) to modify sentences:

    We shall do what we can, *however*.

    Indeed, it appears to be true.

(*d*) to modify phrases:

    It's *altogether* out of the question.

    It went *completely* out of my mind.

When adverbs modify sentences and phrases, they are usually mobile:

    However, we shall do what we can.

    It went out of my mind *completely*.

Their position is fixed, however, when they are used to modify verbs, and when they are used as intensifiers before adjectives and other adverbs:

    He's *very* tall.   He drives *terribly* fast.

    □He's tall very.   □He drives fast terribly.

Exercises

---

1. Underline the adjectives in the following passage, classifying them as either attributive or predicative:

    In the middle of the worst recession of the last fifty years, these three firms have spent between £120,000 and £200,000 on advertising three dictionaries. The dictionaries are new in design and seem well planned. It is clear that they aim to capture new markets.

2. Classify each of the words in italics and explain how each functions:

(a) He was a *friendly* man.
(b) I know him *well*.
(c) Perhaps we *shall* go there for the holidays.
(d) Do you know this *young* man?
(e) Have you a *better* plan?
(f) He is getting *better* but he *must* still rest.
(g) He sang *very loudly*.
(h) I won't, *however*, be able to help you.
(i) *When* will you arrive?
(j) This is my *very best* writing, *although* you *think* it is not *very legible*.

3. Pick out the modals in the following sentences and say whether the modal implies ability, futurity, obligation, permission, possibility or probability:

(a) John can swim but I can't.
(b) May we have some sweets, please?
(c) I shall arrive at 4 p.m.
(d) She must do what she is told.
(e) Perhaps I'll win the car.
(f) Should I write to him?
(g) They couldn't find the way.
(h) It is likely that they will arrive late.

4. Form adverbs from the following list of adjectives and then write a sentence for each adverb. Example:

quick   quickly   He ran home very quickly.

awful	funny	honest	little	strong
bold	good	infinite	notable	wilder

Part 6

Prepositions, conjunctions, exclamations

Prepositions

These are words like 'at', 'by' and 'with' which precede a noun or pronoun. Prepositions can be simple, that is, they may consist of one word only, or complex, that is, consisting of more than one word:

according to   in accordance with

The nine most frequently used prepositions in English are simple:

at by for from in of on to with

Although the above nine prepositions are the most widely occurring in the language, the following are also frequently used:

above	He raised his hand above his head.
across	He ran across the street.
against	He hit his head against a stone wall.
along	He walked slowly along the road.
behind	He walked behind his father.
beneath	He stood beneath the tree to shelter from the rain.
between	Leeds is between York and Manchester.
in front of	I wish he wouldn't sit in front of me! He's too tall!
out of	He came out of that large house.
round	He walked round the town twice.
through	He sailed through the Straits of Gibraltar.
towards	Who is that coming towards us?

Prepositions are followed by object pronouns:

with me/him/her/them

It is also correct to write:

for
to } whom
with

although, in the spoken language, one frequently hears:

for
to   } who
with

It is not possible to list all the many and varied uses of prepositions here, and students are advised to refer to a good dictionary to discover the contexts in which individual prepositions are used. The following examples illustrate some of the uses with which non-native speakers of English have problems.

at   We shall meet *at* home.

We shall meet *at* the cinema.

We shall meet *at* school.

for   We go *for* a walk every day.

We go *for* a drive in the country every day.

We go *for* a ride in the car every day.

in   We walked for hours *in* the rain/*in* the snow.

He was *in* great pain.

We shall get there *in* time.   (that is, with time to spare)

on   We shall get there *on* time.   (that is, at the right time)

We heard the news *on* the radio.

We watched the film *on* television.

It is possible also to say 'on the television' but this implies a particular set. If one is speaking generally, it is not necessary to use 'the'.

Prepositions also occur frequently in idioms. The following five are often misunderstood:

come across: usually means 'meet/find by accident'. We can 'come across' a person or a thing:

I came across an old school friend of ours yesterday.

Did you come across some old photographs in that trunk?

get over: means 'recover from':

I don't think I'll ever get over that accident.

go through: means 'examine carefully':

They go through everyone's baggage at the airport now.

look after: means 'take care of':

She looked after her parents for ten years.

take after: means 'resemble':

That child takes after his father in both looks and temperament.

Conjunctions

Conjunctions are joining words and, in English, we find co-ordinating and subordinating conjunctions.

Co-ordinating conjunctions join units of equal value, for example:

noun + noun	*John* and *Mary*
verb + verb	He *sang* and *danced.*
adjective + adjective	She was *kind* and *gentle.*
phrase + phrase	I put it *on the chair* or *in my bag.*
sentence + sentence	*I saw him* but *he did not see me.*

There is a finite set of co-ordinating conjunctions:

and   but   or   then   yet   either . . . or   neither . . . nor

Subordinating conjunctions introduce clauses and often provide information on when, where, why, how or if an action or event occurs. The most frequently used subordinating conjunctions (also called 'subordinators') are as follows:

after	He arrived *after* I did.
although	*Although* he was tired, he agreed to work late.
as	I told him the news *as* we walked to the house.
as . . . as	He is *as* good now *as* he has always been.
as soon as	He left home *as soon as* he was eighteen.
as if	It looks *as if* she will win the election.
because	I didn't go to the party *because* I wasn't invited.
before	I heard the results *before* you did.
even if	I wouldn't have gone *even if* I had been asked.
even though	We didn't go, *even though* we wanted to.
if	*If* the weather does not improve, the crops will be ruined.
in case	I shall go there *in case* I am needed.
however	He won't succeed *however* hard he tries.
more . . . than	He has *more* money *than* he can ever spend.
since	He has been ill *since* I returned from Canada.
so that	They worked hard *so that* their son could have a good education.
that	I saw *that* he was tired.
though	*Though* she is not rich, she gives a lot of money away.

till	I won't go *till* you give me an answer.
when	Let me know *when* they arrive.
where	He hid the treasure *where* no-one could find it.
wherever	With rings on her fingers and bells on her toes, She shall have music *wherever* she goes.
whether . . . (or not)	I can't decide *whether or not* I should go. I can't decide *whether* I should go (*or not*).
while	Don't get out of bed *while* you have a temperature.
until	I went on working until the library closed.

Exclamations

These words are also often described as 'involuntary interjections'. Usually, exclamations are a feature of speech not writing, and they express a spontaneous response to a person, event or idea. Exclamations can be items like:

Oh!   Hey!   Ouch!   Wow!

which do not have any objective meaning. Occasionally, however, words and phrases are used as exclamations.

The commonest types of exclamation

(*a*) *Pronouns*: can be used to express indignation, disgust, amazement. The speaker's strong feeling is indicated by the use of exclamation marks:

Him!   You!   Them!

Notice that it is the object pronoun that is used in exclamations.

(*b*) *Disparaging words and phrases*: These tend to indicate the speaker's anger with an individual:

(You) Fool!   Idiot!   That silly boy!

(*c*) *'How'* + *word/sentence*: This structure can indicate both pleasure and annoyance:

How lovely!   How you've grown!
How terrible!   How stupid can you get!

(*d*) *'What'* + word/phrase/sentence: This structure can also be used in praise or criticism:

What generosity!   What a mess!
What cheek!   What pleasure you've given us!
What a magnificent building!   What a fool you've made of yourself!

(e) *Rhetorical questions*: These exclamations have the form of questions but are intended to be understood as emphatic statements:

Am I hungry!   (that is, I'm extremely hungry)

Was he cross!   (that is, He was extremely cross)

Were they exhausted!   (that is, They were absolutely exhausted)

(f) *Taboo vocabulary*: In all languages, there are words and expressions that are used to express annoyance, amazement, excitement, frustration which can cause offence to other people. Among such items in English are words associated with religion, such as:

God!   Hell!   Jesus!   Damn!

These words are not taboo when used in a religious context but should be avoided in their exclamatory usage. More acceptable are the American modifications:

Gosh!   Heck!   Gee Whizz!   Darn!

Other taboo items relate to body parts and body functions. A helpful rule to remember is that, in English, discussion of all bodily excretions with the exception of tears and saliva tends to be avoided.

Exercises

1. Insert the correct prepositions in each of the following sentences:
   (a) I am going home —— 5 o'clock.
   (b) We heard the news —— the radio.
   (c) Come —— my office —— 2 o'clock.
   (d) John and Mary looked —— each other —— some time.
   (e) She stood —— her toes and looked —— the hedge.
   (f) I can never see the blackboard because that tall boy always sits —— me.
   (g) He lives in Blockley, a little village —— Oxford and Birmingham.
   (h) She heard —— her son yesterday.
   (i) Can you see who is coming —— us?
   (j) One boy hit the other —— a stone.

2. Underline all the conjunctions in the following passage from *Alice's Adventures in Wonderland*. Say whether the conjunctions are co-ordinating or subordinating.

   Either the well was very deep, or she fell very slowly, because she had plenty of time as she went down to look about her, and to wonder what was going to happen next. First, she tried to look down and make out what she was coming to, but it was too dark to see anything: then she looked at the sides of the well, and noticed that they were filled with cupboards and bookshelves: here and there she saw maps and pictures hung upon pegs. She took down a jar from one of the shelves as she passed: it was labelled "ORANGE MARMALADE", but to her great disappointment it was empty: she did not like to drop the jar for fear of killing somebody underneath, so managed to put it into one of the cupboards as she fell past it.

3. Briefly describe a situation in which each of the following might occur:

(*a*) Them! (*d*) Rubbish! (*g*) Was he angry! (*i*) Not likely!

(*b*) How awful! (*e*) Oh! (*h*) What a mess! (*j*) H'm!

(*c*) Lovely! (*f*) Hey!

Part 7

Sentences in English

NOW THAT WE HAVE EXAMINED word classes, we are in a better position to consider sentences in English. The simplest definition of a sentence is that is begins with a capital letter and ends with a full stop, question mark or exclamation mark. Thus:

I like you.	What a fool I felt!
Come here.	One for all and all for one.
What did you say?	No.

are all sentences but they are clearly different and we can classify them and all other sentences into five main categories.

Types of sentence

1. Declarative sentences
These are sentences which make a statement or an assertion:

I like you.   He is sixteen.   They must not come here.

Declarative sentences can be either affirmative or negative:

I can see you.   I can't see you.

2. Imperative sentences
These are sentences which give orders or make requests:

Stop that at once.	Take these books to my room.
Get out.	Help me, please.

Imperative sentences can be either affirmative or negative:

Put them in there.   Don't put them in there.

3. Interrogative sentences
These ask questions of two types:

(*a*) yes/no questions, that is questions which expect a 'yes' or 'no' answer:

Are you the oldest man here?
Did you hear the noise?
Will you ever come here again?
Wouldn't you like to go there?

(*b*) questions which begin with what?, when?, where?, which?, who?, why? or how? and which expect an answer other than 'yes' or 'no':

> How can I get to the station?
>
> When did you arrive?
>
> Who did that?

Interrogative sentences can be either affirmative or negative:

> Who can play football?   Didn't you hear the bell?

4. Exclamatory sentences

These indicate the speaker's opinion of, or attitude towards their subject matter:

> He's an absolute idiot!
>
> Nobody in his right mind would do such a thing!
>
> What terrible news you've brought!

Exclamatory sentences tend to be affirmative because the speaker is expressing a strong view, but negative exclamations can occur:

> I've never seen such a mess in all my life!
>
> Never in a million years will I speak to him again!

5. Minor sentences

These are sentences which do not contain a finite verb. All sentences, such as those above, which contain a finite verb can be called 'major sentences'. Minor sentences, which can be either affirmative or negative, are common in colloquial speech:

> No.   Not on your life.

in proverbs:

> Better late than the late.   Always a bridesmaid, never a bride.

and in advertising:

> Brand X for beauty and health.   The No. 1 car in its class.

Simple, compound and complex sentences

Apart from the classification discussed above, it is sufficient to distinguish three types of sentence in English, namely *simple*, *compound* and *complex*.

Simple sentences

These contain only one finite verb:

> William the Conqueror *defeated* Harold in 1066.
>
> John *was* a good gardener.

That boy *could run* away.

He *has* always *been* a gentle boy.

Notice that the verb may be made up of one or more auxiliaries as well as a headverb, and that certain adverbs like 'always', 'never' and 'often' can come between the parts of a verb phrase.

Compound sentences

These consist of two or more simple sentences linked by co-ordinating conjunctions:

Harold *defeated* the Vikings but William *defeated* Harold.

You *should* either *do* the job properly or you *should resign*.

He *called* at the house but he *would*n't *come* in.

Notice that in compound sentences shared constituents may be omitted. For example, the last two sentences above might have occurred as:

You should either do the job properly or resign.

He called at the house but wouldn't come in.

In the first of these, 'you should' occurs in both sentences and so can be omitted from the second. Similarly, in the second, 'he' is common to both.

Complex sentences

These consist of one simple sentence (or main clause) and one or more subordinate clauses. In modern descriptions, 'subordinate clauses' are often called 'embedded sentences'. The chief characteristic of subordinate clauses/embedded sentences is that they cannot stand alone because they depend on and are subordinate to a main clause (italicised in the following examples):

When William defeated Harold, *he became king.*

The man who was wearing a black hat *left* when he realised that he was being watched.

Notice that clauses which begin with 'who', 'which' and 'that' often occur within the main clause:

The man left.   *The man* who was wearing a black hat *left*.

As we saw in earlier chapters, English sentences can be analysed in terms of words, phrases and clauses. We have examined words in some depth and are now in a position to consider phrases and clauses more fully.

Phrases

A phrase is a group of words which functions as a unit but which does not contain a finite verb. The commonest types of phrase are:

1. Noun phrases

These are phrases which have a noun as their headword. The units in italics in the following sentences are examples:

The letter arrived yesterday.

The naughty boy called *his teacher/a silly old fool.*

A simple sentence can have up to three noun phrases.

2. Adjective phrases

These are phrases which modify nouns. Like adjectives, they can be either attributive:

The boy, *crying bitterly*, was carried home.

or predicative:

The house seemed *very frightening.*

When an adjective phrase is used attributively, it tends to follow the noun it modifies:

The tree, *bending under the weight of its fruit*, was the first thing he looked at every morning.

Occasionally, however, and more frequently in humorous styles, adjective phrases precede the noun. When this happens they are usually hyphenated:

an *off-the-cuff* remark   an *off-the-shoulder* dress.

3. Predicate phrases

There can only be one finite predicate (or verb) phrase in a simple sentence:

He *will come* tomorrow.

They really *do* not *want* our help.

I *may have been trying* too hard.

4. Adverbial phrases

These units are more mobile than other phrases and it is possible to have several in the same simple sentence:

He learnt to speak English *very quickly.*

He *almost invariably* arrives late.

Next year, we hope to tour Canada *as thoroughly as possible.*

5. Prepositional phrases

These are sometimes described as 'adverbial' because they often tell us when, where, why or how something happened. They can, however, function in other roles. If we compare the following sentences:

She hit the thief *with the handbag.*

and:

She hit the thief *with the scar.*

the phrases in italics are both prepositional (that is, they begin with prepositions) but the first phrase tells us about how the thief was hit. It is therefore adverbial. The second describes the thief and is thus adjectival.

Many modern linguists use the word 'phrase' slightly differently from the way we have described it above. They would describe:

I   John   the boy

as 'noun phrases', and

heard   has heard   may have heard

as 'verb/predicate phrases'. The reason behind this technique is that the items described as 'noun phrases' can all occur in the same linguistic environment:

I ran to catch the train.

John ran to catch the train.

The boy ran to catch the train.

Similarly, the verbal items have a similar pattern of occurrence:

He heard the news.

He has heard the news.

He may have heard the news.

The linguists who refer to one-word items as 'phrases' are concentrating on the functional similarity of the items. We shall, however, only use the term 'phrase' to refer to a unit of more than one word.

Clauses

A clause is a group of words containing a finite verb but usually not capable of occurring in isolation. In complex sentences we can have a *main* clause (that is, the most important clause in the sentence and the one that is most like a complete sentence) and one or more *subordinate* (or 'dependent') clauses. Thus, in the sentence:

He would be very sad if he lived alone.

the main clause is:

He would be very sad

and the subordinate clause is:

if he lived alone.

The three most frequently occurring types of clauses are noun clauses, adjective clauses and adverbial clauses.

1. Noun clauses

It is easiest to illustrate clauses by giving examples:

(a) I shall never forget *what you have done*.

(b) *That porpoises are intelligent* is a well-known fact.

(c) The fact *that you are lazy* is obvious to everyone.

If we look more closely at example (a), we can see that the noun clause can be replaced by 'it' or 'that' or 'you'. When in doubt about how a clause functions, see what you can substitute for it. For example, we might have:

I shall never forget	John.
	him.
	your kindness.
	what you have done.

All of the substitutions are noun-like, so we are dealing with a noun clause. Similar substitutions can be made with example (b):

That porpoises are intelligent	is a well-known fact.
Their intelligence	
That	

Example (c) is not so clear-cut and often causes problems. At first sight, it appears that the clause 'that you are lazy' is telling us more about 'fact' and so a student might suppose that it is an adjective clause. If we look a little closer, however, we see that the clause is not 'describing' the 'fact' but actually telling us what the 'fact' is. We could actually leave out the words 'the fact' and still have a perfectly acceptable sentence:

That you are lazy is obvious to everyone.

We will return briefly to this point when we have described adjective clauses, but the student should be aware that sentences beginning as follows often introduce noun clauses:

The fact that . . .

The idea that . . .

The belief that . . .

The hope that . . .

2. Adjective clauses

As we would expect, these are clauses which describe nouns:

The girl *who is very tall* is my sister.

Notice that the above sentence is very similar in meaning to:

The very tall girl is my sister.

The following sentences illustrate common adjective clauses:

The book *from which you cut that picture* was mine.

The hat *that we put on the scarecrow* belonged to my aunt.

I remember the day *when you had your fifth birthday*.

This last example needs care. Usually 'when' introduces an adverbial clause of time but if 'when' can be replaced by 'on which', it introduces an adjective clause. This point is clear if we compare:

That was the day when I scored 100 runs.

That was the day on which I scored 100 runs.

with:

I was delighted when I scored 100 runs.

□I was delighted on which I scored 100 runs.

It should thus be clear that just as words can function in a variety of roles, the same clause can function differently in different sentences.

Let us now return briefly to the fact that 'that' can introduce both noun and adjective clauses. If we examine the sentences:

The idea *that we can win our match* is very ambitious.

The idea *that John had* was very ambitious.

we see that the first clause equals 'the idea', whereas the second clause describes 'the idea' but does not tell us what 'the idea' is.

3. Adverbial clauses

These are probably the most widely used clauses in the language and can be subdivided into eight types, each of which is illustrated.

(*a*) Clauses of time:

I'll buy the book *when I get some money*.

(*b*) Clauses of place:

Put it back *where you found it*.

(*c*) Clauses of reason:

I bought it *because it was very cheap*.

(*d*) Clauses of manner:

He always did *as he was told*.

(*e*) Clauses of purpose:

I hit him *so that he would never climb trees again.*

(*f*) Clauses of comparison:

He sings *as well as you do.*

(*g*) Clauses of condition:

If you bring this ticket you'll get in free.

(*h*) Clauses of concession:

Although he was poor he was honest.

It is worth stressing again that clauses can function in several different ways and so a clause should not be classified until its role in a specific context has been examined.

Exercises

1. State whether each of the following sentences is declarative, imperative, interrogative or exclamatory. In addition, state also whether each is major or minor.

(*a*) What a fool!

(*b*) What are you doing?

(*c*) Aren't you coming with us?

(*d*) Water boils at 100° centigrade.

(*e*) Who on earth painted that!

(*f*) One man, one vote.

(*g*) Look before you leap.

(*h*) Will you let me have it soon?

(*i*) Take this away at once.

(*j*) In God's court there is no appeal.

2. Examine the following sentences and state whether each group of words in italics is a phrase or a clause.

(*a*) The man, *boastful and argumentative,* was never invited back.

(*b*) *When I scored that goal* I knew we had won the match.

(*c*) Do it *as quickly as possible.*

(*d*) Do it *as often as you can.*

(*e*) The rumour *that he was a fine teacher* reached the school before he did.

(*f*) *On 12 July* we'll have a party.

(*g*) I can't understand *what he says.*

(*h*) *That overflowing river* must have caused *a great deal of damage.*

(*i*) *When opportunity knocks,* don't miss it.

(*j*) Procrastination is *the thief of time.*

3. Pick out the clauses in the following sentences, saying which clauses are main and which subordinate. For example, in the sentence 'Whenever I see him I forget his name.' there are two clauses:

   Main clause: I forget his name
   Subordinate clause: whenever I see him

   (*a*) The boat that I bought was full of holes.
   (*b*) The fact that she was beautiful was stressed.
   (*c*) Come in when I ring the bell.
   (*d*) The man who escaped was wearing a brown coat when I saw him.
   (*e*) He never failed an examination although he rarely did any work.
   (*f*) Meet me after you've finished work.
   (*g*) Do you think he'll come?
   (*h*) That was what he said.
   (*i*) Never say that you'll do something if you have no intention of doing it.
   (*j*) Where did you put the book I gave you?

4. Classify the phrases in italics:

   (*a*) I met him *in Italy*.
   (*b*) *The baby camel* weighed only ten kilos.
   (*c*) He ran *faster than the train*.
   (*d*) She was *unbelievably clever*.
   (*e*) He *may have gone*.
   (*f*) Will you put *that heavy parcel* in my room, please?
   (*g*) *Only the prettiest colours* are chosen.
   (*h*) *In which countries* do people drive *on the left*?
   (*i*) They *must have disappeared*.
   (*j*) Come *into the garden*, Maud.

Part 8

Subject, predicate, object, complement

WHEN STUDYING SENTENCES in English, we can look at the nature of individual units. We can, for example, say that the sentence:

I have seen that student often.

is made up of:

a pronoun:	I
a verb phrase:	have seen
a noun phrase:	that student
an adverb:	often

We could go further and describe each word:

I	=	personal pronoun
have	=	auxiliary verb
seen	=	past participle
that	=	demonstrative determiner
student	=	noun
often	=	adverb

Both these techniques are valid and both shed light on sentences. We are, however, still concentrating on the nature of individual sentence constituents.

Another way of looking at sentences is to focus on the relationships between the units. An analogy may help to make this point clearer. If we consider a female member of the human race, we can give her a class label and call her a 'woman' – that is, we are specifying that she belongs to that class of human beings known as 'women'. Alternatively, we might call her a 'wife' or 'mother' or 'daughter', in which case we would be concentrating on her relationship with others. She is exactly the same individual, but considered from different points of view. Similarly with units of grammar. We can, even without a context, declare that 'a good student' is a noun phrase, but this noun phrase functions differently in each of the following sentences:

A good student always passes examinations.

I interviewed *a good student* today.

I gave *a good student* a prize.

She was *a good student*.

Our next task will be to examine how such units can function in a sentence.

When we study English sentences, we can see that they subdivide and we can label the subdivisions. In such a sentence as:

The old man called.

we can identify two subdivisions, 'The old man' and 'called'. The first part is called a *subject* and the second part a *predicate*. (Fuller definitions will follow. For the moment, we shall simply identify the components.) In the sentence:

The old man called his horse.

we have three units:

Subject:	The old man
Predicate:	called
Object:	his horse.

And in the sentence:

The old man called his horse Trigger.

we can identify four units:

Subject:	The old man
Predicate:	called
Object:	his horse
Complement:	Trigger.

These four units are basic to the analysis of English sentences and can be comprehended by such a formula as:

(Subject) Predicate (Object) (Complement)   *or*:   (S) P (O) (C)

The formula means that although all four units *can* occur in a sentence, it is only necessary to have a predicate. Thus:

Call.   (P)

is a perfectly acceptable sentence, as are:

Call your son.   (P + O)

Call your son John.   (P + O + C)

We call your son John.   (S + P + O + C)

We shall now describe each of these units more precisely.

Subject

The subject of a sentence is the noun-like unit which:

(*a*) usually precedes the predicate in declarative sentences:

Children like sweets. *Children* do not like vegetables.

(*b*) usually occurs within the predicate in interrogative sentences:

Do *children* like sweets? Do *children* not like vegetables?

The only exceptions to this rule occur with 'be' and 'have' when they are used as headverbs:

Children are naughty. *Children* have good eyes.

Are *children* naughty? Have *children* good eyes?

When this happens, the subject simply follows 'be' or 'have'.

(*c*) If the subject is a third person singular subject, for example, 'the boy', 'the girl', 'the stone' or 'he', 'she' or 'it', then it triggers off a modification of non-past verbs. This is clear if we compare, for example, the following:

I remember	The boy remembers	They remember
	He remembers	
I remembered	The little boy remembered	They remembered
	He remembered	

The verb form does not change except in the non-past when there is a third person singular subject.

The commonest types of subject

(1) noun phrases such as 'the boy', 'the man in the moon'

(2) pronouns such as 'he', 'that'

(3) proper names such as 'Muhammad Ali', 'William Wordsworth', 'John'

(4) non-finite verb phrases such as:

To err is human. *Seeing* is believing.

(5) clauses such as:

That rain falls frequently in Britain is a well-known fact.

Why he loves you is a mystery.

(6) 'There' and 'Here' in such sentences as:

There was once a man who lived in Cairo. *Here* is the news.

(7) 'It' in such sentences as:

It is raining. *It* is snowing. *It* is warm and sunny now.

This 'it' is often called a 'dummy' subject because the 'it' does not actually refer to anything in particular. Contrast the uses of 'it' in the following sentences:

The lion is a large cat.   It (that is, the lion) is a carnivore.

It won't stop raining.

As we can see, the first 'it' refers to the lion, but the second 'it' does not stand in for any noun. Its role is merely to fill the subject position in the sentence.

Predicate

This term is used differently by different linguists. For some, the term 'predicate' comprehends both the verb and whatever follows the verb. Thus sentences would be divided as follows:

Subject	Predicate
This young man	minds the sheep.
This young man	ran home quickly.
This young man	was stung by a bee.

In our study, however, the term 'predicate' will apply only to the verbal part of the sentence. Thus, in the above sentences, the predicates would be 'minds', 'ran' and 'was stung'. For us, therefore, the predicate is the verbal unit which possesses the following characteristics:

(*a*) The predicate usually follows the subject in declarative sentences:

The boy *sang* a song.   The boat *sank*.

(*b*) With the exception of 'be' and 'have' predicates need an auxiliary to form negatives and interrogatives. Thus:

The boy *did* not *sing* a song.   *Did* the boat *sink*?

but:

The boy *is* not a shepherd.   The boy *has*n't any money.

Is the boy a shepherd?   *Has* the boy any money?

(*c*) The predicate agrees with its subject in the non-past tense:

I/you/we/they *sink*.   He/she/it/the boat *sinks*.

This agreement means that the base form is used with all subjects except third person singulars. With third person singulars 's' or 'es' is added to the base form of the verb:

| look | He looks well. |
| catch | She catches the ball every time. |

The predicate may be:

(1) *Transitive*, in which case it can take an object:

John rang the bell.

When the predicate is transitive, the sentence can be either 'active' or 'passive':

John rang the bell.   (active)

The bell was rung by John.   (passive)

(2) *Intransitive*, in which case it cannot take an object:

John died.   John ran away.

(3) *Copulative*. This term needs some explanation. If we compare the sentences:

John hit a farmer.   John was a farmer.

we see that, in the first sentence, 'John' and 'the farmer' are different people, whereas in the second sentence 'John' and 'the farmer' refer to the same person. When the verb has an equative function, that is, when it equates the units on either side of it, then the verb is called a *copula*. Here are some sentences involving the commonest copula verbs in English:

Michael is a prince.

The teacher became the president of the United States.

That boy seems a very able student.

Because copula verbs *link* units rather than describing what one unit does to another, we say that copula verbs take 'complements' whereas transitive verbs take 'objects'. (More will be said about transitivity in Part 9.)

Object

The object of a sentence is the noun-like unit which has the following characteristics:

(*a*) It usually follows the predicate:

I saw *five large birds*.

He loves *his brother*.

I didn't hit *him*.

When, for stylistic reasons, the object is emphasised, it precedes the subject as well as the predicate:

Five large birds I saw.

His brother he loves.

This order is, however, rare in prose although it occurs reasonably often in verse:

Two loves I have, of comfort and despair

(Shakespeare, Sonnet 144)

A cold coming we had of it   (T. S. Eliot, *Journey of the Magi*)

(*b*) The object does not occur within the predicate in modern English:

I have seen *it*.

and not:

□I have it seen.

There is an apparent exception to this rule. The object occurs within the predicate in the following sentences:

I had John followed.

I'll have it painted next week.

He has his car washed every day.

Two points become clear, however, when we examine such sentences closely. First, they all involve the auxiliary 'have' and secondly they are all causative – that is, somebody is made to do something. Let us compare:

I had followed John.   I had John followed.

In the first sentence, 'I' did the the following but, in the second, I caused someone else to follow John. You should not confuse these two patterns. The general rule is that the object does not occur within the predicate. (More will be said about 'causatives' in Part 9.)

(*c*) The object never agrees with the predicate:

I see him every day.   She sees him every day.

I see them every day.   She sees them every day.

The commonest types of object

(1) noun phrases such as 'five men', 'five men in a boat'

(2) object pronouns such as 'me', 'him, 'her', 'us', 'whom'

(3) proper nouns such as 'President Lincoln', 'Dar-es-Salaam'

(4) non-finite phrases such as:

He guaranteed *to deliver*.   She promised *to come*.

(5) clauses such as:

He described *how the fight began*.

He didn't know *why he did it*.

He said *that he was tired*.

'That' and 'which'

The last example above allows us to make two further points about objects. The first relates to the relative pronouns 'that' and 'which'. These are optional when a clause occurs after a verb of saying (for example, 'say', 'remark'), thinking ('think', 'wonder'), and mental processes ('realise', 'remember'):

> He said (that) he was tired.
>
> He thought (that) she would come.
>
> He realised (that) he had been wrong.

and also when the clause describes a noun:

> the hat (that/which) I bought   the man (whom/that) I saw

Direct and indirect speech

The second point relates to direct and indirect speech. When the exact words of a speaker are given, we refer to this as *direct speech*. Thus:

> 'I am very tired,' said John.
>
> John shouted: 'Don't get out of the car.'
>
> 'What do you want?' asked John.

Notice that the exact words are quoted within pairs of quotation marks and, if the attribution occurs before the exact words, we have:

> John said/shouted/asked: '. . . . . .'.

When the attribution follows the exact words, we have:

> '. . . . . .' said/shouted/asked John.

If the exact words are not used when speech is reported, as in:

> John said that he was very tired.
>
> John shouted that they should not get out of the car.
>
> John asked him what he wanted.

then we refer to this as *indirect speech* or 'reported speech' and certain rules apply. The speech is put one step further into the past:

> 'I love you,' said John.   'I loved you,' said John.
>
> John said that he loved her.   John said that he had loved her.

and, as we can see from the above examples, first and second person pronouns are changed to third person pronouns.

The indirect object

Occasionally, with certain verbs such as 'build', 'give', 'make', 'send', 'sell', 'write', it looks as if we have two objects in one sentence:

> He built *her* a lovely kennel.
>
> He gave *his mother* some flowers.

He made *me* a boomerang.

He wrote *his father* a very angry letter.

It will be noticed that the units in italics are the recipients of an action and also that the same ideas can be expressed as follows:

He built a lovely kennel *for her.*

He gave some flowers *to his mother.*

He made a boomerang *for me.*

He wrote a very angry letter *to his father.*

The term *indirect object* is applied to the italicised units. An indirect object is the beneficiary or recipient of an action. It can be recognised (i) by its position in that it immediately precedes the direct object:

He sold *me* a very bad car.

or (ii) by the fact that it is preceded by 'to' or 'for':

He sold a very bad car *to me.*

Complement

This is a unit which, as its name suggests, is needed to 'complete' a sentence. Complements most frequently occur after 'be', 'become', 'grow' and 'seem'. The complement has the following characteristics:

(*a*) It normally follows the predicate:

    It was *my fault.*   John grew *angry.*

If the sentence has an object, the complement follows the object:

They called the pudding '*Peach Melba*'.

They made Ronald Reagan *President.*

Notice the difference between *indirect object + object* and *object + complement:*

    I gave him ten francs.   him $\neq$ ten francs

    I called him a fool.   him = a fool.

(*b*) It never occurs within the predicate:

    They don't seem *the same.*   He is not getting *any younger.*

(*c*) Since the complement and the subject can refer to the same entity, it sometimes happens that the subject, predicate and complement are in agreement:

    It is not my book.   They are not my books.

It is also possible, however, to have sentences like:

    It is not my concern.   They are not my concern.

In other words, the concordial agreement is obligatory between a subject and a non-past verb form:

He seems tired.   They seem tired.

but only occurs in particular contexts with complements:

He is a fool.   He seems the same.
They are fools.   They seem the same.

It is perhaps worth stressing at this point that agreement seems to occur frequently with complements because of two factors: (i) the units on both sides of the copula refer to the same entity:

Harry is a baker.

and (ii) 'be' is the most frequently used copula and it has a wider range of agreement than any other verb in English. Whereas with all other verbs, agreement only ever occurs between a third person singular subject and a non-past form of the verb, with 'be' we find the following pattern:

I am tired.   I/he/she/it was tired.
You/we/they are tired.   You/we/they were tired.
He/she/it is tired.

The commonest types of complement

(1) Adjectives:

He is *happy*.

(2) Noun phrases:

He is *a carpenter*.   He called his son *a fool*.

(3) Proper names:

That is *Michael Smith*.   He called his son *Brian*.

(4) Preposition phrases:

He was *in hospital*.   The seed grew *into an oak*.

(5) Non-finite phrases:

The problem was *deciding its value*.
The future seemed *to depend on him*.

(6) Clauses:

A corollary to this theorem is *that parallelograms on equal bases and between the same parallel lines are equal in area*.
His chief strength was *that he knew his weaknesses*.

(7) Adverbs:

The fire is *out*.   The gas is *on*.   The game is *off*.

(8) A pronoun can occur as complement, as in:

The point is *this*.   It's *me*.

Who is *he*?   Which is *which*?

but pronouns are much less likely to occur as complements than as subjects and objects.

Exercises

1. Describe the function of each of the units in italics in the following sentences:

   (*a*) Who is *that*?
   (*b*) I want *a piece of cake*.
   (*c*) *He* called *his brother*.
   (*d*) He called his brother *a genius*.
   (*e*) We *shall be leaving* soon.
   (*f*) What *has* he *done*?
   (*g*) *What he said* was unprintable.
   (*h*) *Will* you *be coming* too?
   (*i*) *How to speak clearly* is the subject of elocution.
   (*j*) Why did they elect him *president*?

2. Pick out the subjects and objects in the following passage and say whether each is a noun phrase, a pronoun, a proper noun, a non-finite phrase or a clause:

   John was a determined young man. He studied hard and played football like a professional. His ambition was to play centre forward for Manchester United and then to teach History in a good school. What made John different from the other boys was his ambition. He wanted to be best at everything. Hard work seemed a delight and success gave him great joy.

3. Underline and classify the objects and complements in the following sentences:

   (*a*) He made me a bow and arrow.
   (*b*) He called me his friend.
   (*c*) Give me some cake, please.
   (*d*) He become a pilot.
   (*e*) Don't tell him the bad news yet.
   (*f*) Make him the captain.
   (*g*) He wanted to bet on the black mare.
   (*h*) He wanted ice-cream.
   (*i*) He seemed very gentle.
   (*j*) The fire was out.

4. Pick out all the indirect objects and the complements in the following sentences:

   (*a*) Don't send him any.
   (*b*) Make him some tea.
   (*c*) Try to tell her that.
   (*d*) What's that?
   (*e*) She said that she arrived home last night.
   (*f*) The elected members were from the same town.
   (*g*) He gave us roses in the summer.
   (*h*) He grew irritable in the summer.
   (*i*) Give that to me.
   (*j*) Drop him a note.

5. Underline the predicates in the following sentences:

   It should have been a good day. Everyone thought that the good weather would last until Friday. It was still only Wednesday and the sky was black and threatening. Thunder clouds had been building up since noon and now the distant rumbles were no longer so distant.

   'I hate storms,' said Jane.

   'Me too,' answered Michael. 'You have to admit though that they can be very exciting.'

Part 9

Transitivity

IN PARTS 5 AND 8 WE REFERRED to active and passive sentences. We can now deal more fully with this important area of English grammar.

It is not uncommon in modern descriptions of English to classify verbs according to whether they require one, two or three nominals. (We will use the term *nominal* to comprehend nouns, pronouns, proper names and noun phrases.) Verbs such as 'arrive' and 'die' require only one nominal:

Summer has arrived.   John died.

These have been called 'one-place verbs' and they are intransitive. That means they do not take an object. Other verbs like 'kill' and 'see' tend to require two nominals:

John killed the lion.   He saw that film.

These are called 'two-place verbs' because they take a subject and an object. Two-place verbs are therefore transitive. Still other verbs like 'give' and 'write' often co-occur with three nominals – a subject, an object and an indirect object:

John gave her a present.   He wrote a letter to his parents.

These three-place verbs are also transitive.

If we look at sentences containing transitive verbs, we find that they can occur in two types of related sentences, traditionally called *active* and *passive* voice, thus:

John killed the lion.   (active)

The lion was killed by John.   (passive)

John gave her a present.   (active)

A present was given to her by John.   (passive)

We say that a sentence is 'active' or 'in the active voice' when the subject of the sentence is the agent of the action. When the subject receives the action, we say the sentence is 'passive' or 'in the passive voice'. Notice that the related active and passive sentences:

The boy saw the girl.

and:

The girl was seen (by the boy).

mean approximately the same but that they differ in a number of ways:

(*a*) The object of the active sentence becomes the subject of the passive sentence.

(*b*) The verb in the active sentence is changed into a form of 'be' plus the past participle of the headverb. Thus:

John loves Mary.	*becomes*	Mary is loved by John.
John loved Mary.		Mary was loved by John.
John loved the children.		The children were loved by John.

(*c*) The active sentence must have at least two nominals, but the passive sentence may only have one:

John killed Mary.	Mary was killed.

In other words, in passive sentences, it is not necessary to mention who performed the action. This means that the passive voice is often selected when the speaker does not wish to specify the agent:

Mary was hit.

The buildings were ransacked.

The money was stolen.

(*d*) Active sentences put the main emphasis on the agent; passive sentences put the main emphasis on the recipient of the action.

Pseudo-intransitive sentences

A number of transitive verbs such as 'eat', 'shave', 'write' frequently occur in sentences that *look* intransitive, as is clear if we compare the sentences in columns 'A' and 'B':

A	B
They eat at seven.	They eat their main meal at seven.
He shaves every morning.	He shaves his chin every morning.
She wrote when she was young.	She wrote books when she was young.

The 'A' sentences have been called *pseudo-intransitive* because they look like such intransitive sentences as:

C

They arrived at seven.

He struggles every morning.

She died when she was young.

The difference between the verbs in the 'A' and the 'C' sentences is that one can retrieve an object for the 'A' set by putting 'what' or 'whom' after the verb:

They eat what?   Their dinner?   Their tea?

It does not make sense to put 'what' or 'whom' after an intransitive verb.

Pseudo-intransitive sentences serve a stylistic function similar to passives. With passive sentences, we do not have to mention the agent:

The book was written (by X).

whereas, with pseudo-intransitive sentences, we do not have to mention the object:

He writes (for example, books, articles, letters, stories for women's magazines).

Ergative sentences

If we now look at such pairs of sentences as:

(a) John rings the bell at noon.

(b) The bell rings at noon.

we can see that they are related and that 'rings' in (a) is transitive (it takes the object 'the bell'.) The verb in (b) is not transitive, however. Nor is it pseudo-intransitive. We cannot get an answer to such questions as:

The bell rings what?/whom?

There are quite a number of verbs in English which can occur both transitively and intransitively:

John opened the door.   John broke the cup.
The door opened.   The cup broke.

All such verbs involve change, either a change in position:

close   move   open   shut   start   stop

or a change in state:

boil   break   change   cook   split   tear

Some linguists use the term *ergative* to describe the relationship that exists between such sentences as:

John stopped the car.   The car stopped.

The word 'ergative' comes from a Greek verb meaning 'cause something to happen', 'bring something about', and, in the above sentences, John clearly caused the car to stop. For most students, it is not necessary to remember the term 'ergative' but it is very worthwhile to realise that ergative or causative relationships underlie a large number of stylistically related sets of sentences. We shall illustrate these relationships by drawing attention to the facts that:

(1) As we have seen, the same verb can occur in related pairs of sentences:

> John stewed the meat for two hours.
>
> The meat stewed for two hours.

(2) Morphologically related verbs can occur in a causatively connected set:

> The mother is laying the baby on the bed.
>
> The baby is lying on the bed.
>
> The woodcutter will fell that tree.
>
> That tree will fall.

(3) Morphologically distinct verbs can occur in a similar relationship:

> John killed Peter.   (that is, John caused Peter to die)
>
> Peter died.

(4) Large numbers of adjectives and related verbs can occur in causatively related sentences:

> Brand X makes your whole wash white.
>
> Brand X whitens your whole wash.
>
> Brand Y keeps your hands soft.
>
> Brand Y softens your hands.

Such related sentences often occur in advertising language, but the relationship between adjectives and causative verbs is not limited to this genre as can be clearly seen from the following list:

Adjectives	Verbs
active	activate
beautiful	beautify
better	improve/better
cool	cool
dead	kill/deaden
dry	dry
large/larger	enlarge
low/lower	lower/reduce
wider	widen

Synthetic and analytic structures

If we examine another few pairs of related sentences, we can draw the reader's attention to a further linguistic phenomenon:

> (a) John improved his property.
>
> (b) John made his property better.

(*a*) Mary lengthened her skirt.

(*b*) Mary made her skirt longer.

(*a*) Swan cream softens your skin.

(*b*) Swan cream makes your skin soft/softer.

The (*a*) sentences are shorter and more succinct than the (*b*) sentences. The verbs in the (*a*) sentences are called *synthetic* verbs because they combine or synthesise two or more words into one, thus:

improve = make better

lengthen = make longer

soften   = make soft/softer

The (*b*) sentences are called *analytic* because the meaning is more clearly apparent. Analytic structures are more common in speech than in writing, and synthetic structures are more common in American English than in British English. Synthetic verbs are more economical than analytic expressions, as we can see if we compare columns 'A' and 'B':

A	B
hospitalise	put into hospital
placate	make more amenable
verify	check the truth of

Exercises

1. Pick out the transitive verbs in the following sentences. For each transitive verb found, write three other sentences, indicating the direct object in each sentence.

   (*a*) John died very suddenly.
   (*b*) John sang three ballads.
   (*c*) John refereed the match.
   (*d*) John played in the tournament.
   (*e*) Where did you put my books?
   (*f*) When did he arrive here?
   (*g*) Have your heard the news?
   (*h*) I don't believe in such things.
   (*i*) We won't go there again.
   (*j*) We always catch the 9 o'clock bus.

2. Say whether the verbs in the following sentences are used transitively, pseudo-intransitively or intransitively.

   (*a*) Who rang?
   (*b*) The stones rolled down the hill.

(c) I cooked the dinner yesterday.
(d) The meat will burn if you don't turn it.   (2 verbs)
(e) The chair broke.
(f) The man moved the stool with his foot.
(g) We always dine at noon.
(h) We often sleep at noon.
(i) We never take a walk at noon.
(j) What's cooking? It smells very good.   (2 verbs)

3. There are no agents in the following sentences. Write parallel sentences containing an agent and say (1) which sentence seems more explicit and (2) what seems to be gained by not having an agent. Example:

> The train stopped.
> *Parallel sentence*: The driver stopped the train.

The second sentence is more explicit. The first sentence is ambiguous. The train could have been stopped by the driver, by a mechanical fault, by a landslide, etc. If a speaker or writer wishes to be mysterious, he often uses sentences where the agent is not mentioned. Students might keep this in mind when they are reading detective stories.

(a) The door opened slowly.
(b) The kettle boiled.
(c) My shirt washed well.
(d) The sheep went into the pen.
(e) That chicken has been cooking for two hours.
(f) The money disappeared.
(g) The car started with a jerk.
(h) My dress tore.
(i) His behaviour has changed.
(j) Poor John died.

4. Write analytic equivalents of the following sentences. Example:

> John widened his path.   John made his path wider.

(a) The old lady shortened her curtains.
(b) John heated the milk.
(c) The law has legalised this type of behaviour.
(d) He falsified the evidence.
(e) Cruelty seems to brutalise people.
(f) He will have to be hospitalised.
(g) The mother fed the baby.
(h) Omo brightens your whole wash.
(i) This glass magnifies objects.
(j) He detonated the device.

5. Write synthetic equivalents of the following sentences:

(*a*) We went to the market on foot.
(*b*) He put the information in a file.
(*c*) She put wallpaper on the room.
(*d*) They used sandpaper to make the wood smooth.
(*e*) She gave food to the children.

Part 10

Idioms

ALL LANGUAGES USE WORDS AND PHRASES in a non-literal way. In English, for example, if we say 'The hole gaped' we are using 'gaped' non-literally or metaphorically. Metaphors are found in all types of speech and writing. Some, like 'the eye of a needle', are so commonly used that we no longer think of them as metaphorical. A few even tend to oust the literal. This is the case with 'petrify', which literally means 'turn to stone' but is much more commonly understood in contemporary English as 'frighten'.

Idioms are like metaphors in that they are examples of the non-literal use of language. They warrant a special section, however, because non-native speakers often misuse them and native speakers tend to overuse them. Idioms are acceptable in colloquial speech but since they are often imprecise and hackneyed, it is best to avoid them in writing.

An idiom can be defined as a group of words whose meaning cannot be grasped from the normal meanings of the words that make up the piece of language. A few examples will illustrate this. If we look at:

| kick the bucket | *meaning* | die |
| spill the beans | | confess, reveal information |

we cannot arrive at the meanings of 'die' or 'confess' by knowing the meanings of 'kick', 'bucket', 'spill' or 'beans'.

There are many kinds of idiom in English but we can subdivide them into the following six main categories:

(1) *Noun phrases*:
The commonest idioms in this category are phrases like:

a red herring	*meaning*	a false trail
a wild goose chase		a fruitless errand
the grass roots		the majority of the people
the nitty gritty		the crux of the matter

(2) *Preposition + noun phrase*:

in the nick of time	*meaning*	without a second to spare
by the skin of his teeth		with nothing to spare
by leaps and bounds		with amazing speed
to all intents and purposes		as far as we can judge

(3) *Verb + noun phrase*:

burn one's boats	*meaning*	destroy one's means of escape
bury the hatchet		agree to forget past problems
smell a rat		notice something suspicious
bite the dust		die

(4) *Verb + preposition + noun phrase*:

be at sixes and sevens	*meaning*	be confused or not in agreement
fly off the handle		get angry
go round in circles		act in a confused manner
throw in the towel/sponge		admit defeat

(5) *Adjective + adjective*:

hard and fast	*meaning*	unchangeable
rough and ready		not well organised
spick and span		extremely tidy
thick and fast		very quickly

(6) *Verb + preposition*:

give in	*meaning*	yield
put down		kill (an animal)
take in		cheat, fool
take off		imitate

Having given examples of the main categories of idiom in English, we are now in a position to comment on their main features and characteristics:

(1) Idioms range from the totally opaque to the reasonably transparent. That means that some idioms are less easily deciphered than others. An idiom like 'a red herring' meaning 'a false trail' is opaque unless one happens to know that smoked herrings were once used to put dogs off the scent of their quarry. An idiom like 'burn the midnight oil' meaning 'work very late' is, however, more easily interpreted and so it is said to be 'transparent'.

(2) Idioms are usually fixed with regard to number:

kick the bucket	*and not*	□kick the buckets
a wild goose chase		□wild geese chase/chases

with regard to the use of determiners:

a lame duck	*and not*	□the lame duck
carry the can		□carry a can

with regard to word order:

spick and span	*and not*	□span and spick
the nitty gritty		□the gritty nitty

with regard to comparatives and superlatives:

a blind date	*and not*	□a blinder date
red tape		□redder/reddest tape

and often too with regard to passives:

he spilt the beans	*and not*	□the beans were spilt by him
he footed the bill		□the bill was footed by him

There is a tendency for the more transparent idioms, such as:

hit your head against a wall

meaning 'make no impression on someone or something', to allow some modification. Thus we can also have:

hit your head against a brick wall

bang your head against a brick wall

knock your head against a *stone* wall

With more opaque idioms, however, any alteration in form tends to emphasise the literal as opposed to the idiomatic meaning of the group of words.

(3) Colours are sometimes used in a quasi-idiomatic way. Thus 'red hair' is not red and 'white coffee' and 'white elephants' are not white.

In summary, one can say that idioms occur along a continuum ranging from the totally opaque and unchanging:

bark up the wrong tree   *meaning*   reach the wrong conclusion

to the more transparent and more flexible:

work like a horse   work like a slave   work like an ox

It is never safe to translate idioms from one language to another. The French idioms

Tout s'avise à qui pain faut.   A bon chat bon rat.

become in English:

Necessity is the mother of invention.   Tit for tat.

and not 'People who need bread will be innovative' or 'To a good cat a good rat.' The more frozen and opaque an idiom is in one language, the less likely is it to translate into another.

Exercises

1. Using a dictionary such as the *Oxford Dictionary of Current Idiomatic English* find out the meaning of the folowing idioms:

   (*a*) soft-soap someone
   (*b*) Let sleeping dogs lie.
   (*c*) a cold war
   (*d*) a rolling stone
   (*e*) a jack of all trades
   (*f*) as mad as a hatter
   (*g*) as like as two peas
   (*h*) back the wrong horse
   (*i*) put up with
   (*j*) go into the red

2. Complete the following idioms and say what each one means:

   (*a*) get it from the horse's . . . . .
   (*b*) as old as the . . . . .
   (*c*) get into . . . water
   (*d*) be a . . . . Samaritan
   (*e*) bend the . . . . . to suit oneself
   (*f*) have a . . . . to pick with someone
   (*g*) keep a . . . profile
   (*h*) go back to the . . . . . roots
   (*i*) bury the . . . .
   (*j*) clear the . . .

3. In each of the following phrases, a colour is used quasi-idiomatically. Say what each phrase means and find out if any other word could replace the colour:

   (*a*) paint the town red
   (*b*) red tape
   (*c*) a red letter day
   (*d*) a brown study
   (*e*) a white lie
   (*f*) a white elephant
   (*g*) black market
   (*h*) be in the black
   (*i*) be in the pink
   (*j*) have the blues

Part 11

Discourse analysis

AS WE HAVE SEEN IN EARLIER CHAPTERS, it is not easy to offer neat, simple definitions of a sentence. We have agreed that a sentence begins with a capital letter and ends with a full stop; and we have also seen that sentences can be simple, compound or complex and that they can be either major or minor. So far, we have looked only at sentences and at the units which compose them. We shall now change our perspective and look at how sentences in continuous prose are linked. This is best done by examining a very simple passage such as the following:

JOURNEYS OF DISCOVERY

In earlier days it was claimed that the earth was flat. Even so, there were some navigators who behaved as if they believed otherwise. There was clearly only one way to disprove the claim. If the earth was not flat, it should be possible to sail round it, returning to one's original starting point. If, on the other hand, the earth really *was* flat, such a voyage would mean certain death. In view of the risks involved, it is perhaps surprising that anyone undertook such a journey. Yet, if records are to be believed, there were many travellers willing to undertake it.

The above passage is a very ordinary piece of prose containing seven sentences. Each sentence is grammatically complete and could be interpreted even if it appeared out of context. In another way, however, each sentence is more easily comprehended *within* its context. This is because in all prose passages sentences interact to produce a coherent whole. In our passage, for example, the cohesion depends on such factors as:

Consistency of ideas
Each sentence expands and complements each of the others.

Consistency of vocabulary
No word strikes the reader as being unusual, unacceptable or even unexpected. In addition, several words belong to what we can call a 'lexical set' of sailing: 'navigators', 'sail', 'starting point', 'voyage', 'journey', 'travellers'. By 'lexical set' we mean that in the discussion of any given topic, certain words are likely to occur. Thus, on the subject of football, we would expect a lexical set containing such items as

'ball', 'kick', 'goal', 'referee' and 'whistle'. Similarly, in any discussion of war, we might predict the occurrence of such a lexical set as 'death', 'destruction', 'bullets', 'gun', 'blood' and 'suffering'.

Consistency of time reference

In our passage, the period referred to is the past and so all our finite verbs are in the past tense: 'was', 'were', 'behaved', 'believed', etc. It is unusual in a well-written passage to find changes in tense. The obvious exception to this rule may occur when a writer introduces direct speech into the narrative.

Consistency of tone

The passage is a simple narrative. There are no unexpected changes of style. Often too, a passage will utilise the same 'voice' so that active sentences are likely to predominate in story-telling, whereas passive sentences are often a feature of scientific prose.

Links

In addition to the features of consistency listed above, the cohesion of the passage is increased by the links that occur between the sentences. In particular, we can highlight:

Even so . . . . . otherwise.

. . . clearly . . . . . the claim.

If . . .

If, on the other hand . . . such . . .

Yet, if . . .

All sentences in a prose passage are linked by such items as the above, although individual writers will select linking items which best suit their individual purposes. Generalising, however, we can mention the seven most frequently occurring types of sentence linkage in contemporary English:

(*a*) Verb substitutes, especially auxiliaries and 'do'. In sentences such as:

(i)   Who came in?   (ii)   John did.

the verb 'did' in (ii) can only be fully understood with reference to the verb in (i). Similarly, in such a conversation as:

'I'll never be able to swim,' said John.

'Of course you will,' answered his father. 'You'll just have to try harder.'

the 'will' is interpreted as 'will be able to swim' and the 'try' is understood to mean 'try to swim'. Thus, all the direct speech sentences are linked to the first sentence by verb substitutes.

(*b*) Noun substitutes, especially personal and demonstrative pronouns and expressions like 'the former' and 'such'. Again, illustrative sentences will clarify this:

> John Smith was tall, dark and handsome. *He* was only twenty-four but *he* was already rich and employed two secretaries. *These* were called Janet and Jane and *they* worked on alternate days. *The former* was beautiful and exceptionally competent. *The latter* was merely beautiful.

In the above passage, the noun substitutes have been italicised. 'He' is a substitute for 'John Smith'; 'these' and 'they' stand for 'Janet' and 'Jane'; 'the former' refers to 'Janet' and 'the latter' to 'Jane'. Such noun substitutes are a common feature in all connected speech and prose.

(*c*) Items which imply a time sequence; for example, 'first', 'last', 'secondly', 'finally', 'then', 'and then', 'in conclusion', 'at that time', 'in the past', 'in the future', 'earlier', 'formerly', 'meanwhile' and 'afterwards'.

(*d*) Items which imply alternatives; for example, 'either ... or', 'neither ... nor', 'on the other hand', 'or else', 'however', 'yet' and 'otherwise'.

(*e*) Items which imply cause and effect: for example, 'because', 'for that reason', 'therefore', 'so' and 'thus'.

(*f*) Items that imply conditions; for example, 'if', 'must therefore', 'unless' and 'on condition that'.

(*g*) Items which imply addition; for example, 'and', 'furthermore', 'in addition', 'as well as', 'together with' and 'in conclusion'.

Some of the above links are to be found in all passages of contemporary prose that a student might care to examine. They give cohesion to a passage and help to distinguish integrated prose from lists of sentences.

Exercises

1. The following passage is taken from a newspaper. List all the features that contribute to the cohesion of the passage.

   Metro Toronto police have charged New York Yankees' superstar outfielder David Winfield after a ball he threw struck and killed a gull at last night's American League baseball game against the Toronto Blue Jays.

   The incident occurred after the Yankee outfielders completed their warm-up throws as the Blue Jays came to the plate in the bottom of the fifth inning.

Winfield, 28, threw the ball in the direction of a Yankees' batboy, but it struck the gull.

2. Using items of linkage, mould the following ten sentences into one coherent passage.

(1) John Smith loved only two people: John Smith and Mary Brown.

(2) Mary Brown loved John Smith.

(3) Mary Brown worried about John Smith's character.

(4) Mary Brown suspected that John Smith might turn into a recluse.

(5) Mary Brown worried that John Smith would become increasingly alienated from people.

(6) Mary Brown worried that Mary Brown would lose contact with Mary Brown's family and friends.

(7) Mary Brown worried that the children Mary Brown and John Smith might have would be isolated from society.

(8) John Smith could not understand why Mary Brown worried so much.

(9) John Smith could not understand why Mary Brown worried so much about people John Smith felt were not worth worrying about.

(10) John Smith told Mary Brown that Mary Brown should stop worrying.

3. Linkage occurs naturally in speech and prose but it is cultivated by writers of literature. In most verse, for example, we note that, in addition to such items of linkage as mentioned in Part 11, we find linkage also in the form of rhythm, rhyme and alliteration. List all the features of linkage that occur in the following stanzas:

(a)   I wonder do you feel to-day
    As I have felt, since, hand in hand,
    We sat down on the grass, to stray
    In spirit better through the land,
    This morn of Rome and May?

                            Robert Browning

(b)   I have been here before,
    But when or how I cannot tell:
    I know the grass beyond the door,
    The sweet keen smell,
    The sighing sound, the lights around the shore.

                            D. G. Rossetti

(*c*)   For nature, heartless, witless nature,
       Will neither care nor know
       What stranger's feet may find the meadow
       And trespass there and go,
       Nor ask amid the dews of morning
       If they are mine or no.

A. E. Housman

Answers to exercises

With some exercises, it is possible to have more than one correct answer. We have chosen the simplest option.

Part 2

1. *Nouns*: man   Weatherill   contraption   sportsfields   device
   Bob   Frost   Mr. Winter   manager   men   rain   flood
   orders   clubs   Motomops   groundsman   Fenners   Cambridge
   cricket   season.
   Pronouns: it   they   They   it.

2. (*a*) adverb   (*b*) adjective   (*c*) preposition   (*d*) verb; adjective
   (*e*) verb; noun   (*f*) pronoun   (*g*) pronoun; determiner
   (*h*) exclamation; pronoun; pronoun   (*i*) noun   (*j*) preposition.

3. *Adjectives*:   intelligent   elder   good   perfect   other   naughty.
   Adverbs: highly   fluently   invariably   faster   often   always.

4. (*a*) noun   (*b*) adverb   (*c*) noun   (*d*) verb   (*e*) adjective
   (*f*) noun   (*g*) adjective   (*h*) adverb   (*i*) noun   (*j*) preposition
   (*k*) noun   (*l*) adverb.

Part 3

1. (*a*) at the station   on the way   to London
   (*b*) The young man   singing loudly   into the busy street
   (*c*) At what time   the London train
   (*d*) in a bag   at the bottom   of the garden
   (*e*) To become a dancer   his greatest dream

2. (*a*) that they passed on the stairs on the way to their room   (passed)
   (*b*) which was on the third floor   (was)
   (*c*) if you had good eyes   (had)
   (*d*) that smugglers used to hide their contraband there   (used)
   (*e*) if that story was true   (was)
   (*f*) although most of the locals believed it   (believed)

3. The tale implies that a bride must ask permission to use the resources she finds when she comes to live with her husband. This

principle is directly stated in the claim: 'That is why, my lord, the bride does not get anything for herself.' If she wants anything, she tells the people of the house what she needs and they get it for her.

4 sentences	The tale . . . husband.	'That is . . . herself.'
	This principle . . . claim:	If she wants . . . for her.
6 clauses:	that the bride . . . resources	why the bride . . . herself
	she finds	if she wants anything
	when she comes to live	what she needs

Part 4

1. Manchester United (proper)   display (common)   Saturday (proper)   cup (common)   game (common)   pitch (common) spectators (common)   players (common)   game (common) entertainment (common)   excitement (common)   finish (common).

2. *beauty*: abstract   *brick*: concrete   *cat*: concrete   *courage*: abstract *leisure*: abstract   *lettuce*: concrete   *loaf*: concrete   *love*: abstract *wealth*: abstract   *wheel*: concrete   *worm*: concrete   *worry*: abstract.

3. (*a*) He   (*b*) They   (*c*) her   (*d*) They   (*e*) his.

4. (*a*) pronoun   (*b*) determiner   (*c*) determiner; determiner   (*d*) pronoun; determiner   (*e*) pronoun   (*f*) determiner   (*g*) pronoun; determiner   (*h*) determiner   (*i*) determiner   (*j*) determiner; pronoun.

5. (*a*) The (article); his (possessive)   (*b*) This (demonstrative); no (indefinite)   (*c*) your (possessive)   (*d*) Six (number); a (article) (*e*) Few (indefinite); the (article).

Part 5

1. worst (attributive)   last (attributive)   fifty (attributive)   three (attributive)   three (attributive)   new (predicative)   clear (predicative)   new (attributive).

2. (*a*) *friendly*: adjective, describes 'man'
   (*b*) *well*: adverb, modifies 'know'
   (*c*) *shall*: modal verb, auxiliary of 'go'
   (*d*) *young*: adjective, describes 'man'
   (*e*) *better*: adjective, describes 'plan'
   (*f*) *better*: adverb, modifies 'is getting'; *must*: modal verb, auxiliary of 'rest'

(*g*) *very*: adverb, modifies 'loudly'; *loudly*: adverb, modifies 'sang'

(*h*) *however*: adverb, modifies sentence

(*i*) *when*: adverb, interrogative of time

(*j*) *very*: adverb, modifies 'best'; *best*: adjective, describes 'writing'; *although*: adverb, modifies sentence; *think*: verb, predicate of clause: *very*: adverb, modifies 'legible'; *legible*: adjective, describes 'writing'.

3. (*a*) can (ability); can't (ability)   (*b*) May (permission)   (*c*) shall (futurity)   (*d*) must (obligation)   (*e*) 'll (possibility)   (*f*) Should (obligation)   (*g*) couldn't (ability)   (*h*) will (probability).

4.
awful:	awfully	He is awfully fat.
bold:	boldly	She stared boldly at the burglar.
funny:	funnily	Funnily enough, I did not recognise you.
good:	well	They sing well.
honest:	honestly	I honestly don't know what happened.
infinite:	infinitely	The speech was infinitely boring.
little:	less	He earns less than his son.
notable:	notably	He's a notably fine architect.
strong:	strongly	No matter how strongly he pulled, the animal refused to move.
wilder:	more wildly	They have been behaving even more wildly since their father arrived.

Part 6

1. (*a*) at (*b*) on (*c*) to, at (*d*) at, for (*e*) on, over (*f*) in front of (*g*) between (*h*) from (*i*) towards (*j*) with.

2. Either . . . or (co-ordinating)   because (subordinating)   as (subordinating)   and (co-ordinating)   and (co-ordinating)   but (co-ordinating)   then (co-ordinating)   and (co-ordinating)   that (subordinating)   and (co-ordinating)   and (co-ordinating)   and (co-ordinating)   as (subordinating)   but (co-ordinating)   so (co-ordinating)   as (subordinating).

3. (*a*) *Them*!   This could be used to express your dislike for some people. If two people were always being held up to you as models of good behaviour, you might say: 'Them!' or 'Them again!' to express your annoyance.

(*b*) *How awful*!   This might be used by someone who had just been told of a very serious accident.

(*c*) *Lovely*!   Tone of voice is important when interpreting this exclamation.

It could be used positively by someone commenting on a beautiful picture. It could be used negatively by someone looking at a mess and saying: 'Lovely!' with sarcasm in their voice.

(*d*) *Rubbish*!   This might occur as a direct contradiction of a preceding remark. If, for example, two teachers were discussing a badly behaved student and one said: 'I don't think he means any harm,' the second might reply: 'Rubbish!'

(*e*) *Oh*!   This occurs as an exclamation of surprise, delight, shock or amazement. If someone appears unexpectedly and frightens a person, that person might say: 'Oh!'

(*f*) *Hey*!   This is used as a means of calling someone or attracting someone's attention. It is usually impolite. If you saw someone doing something that he shouldn't, you might call out: 'Hey!' It may also be used as an expression of surprise.

(*g*) *Was he angry*!   This could occur as part of a story relating how someone had become very angry indeed.

(*h*) *What a mess*!   This might be used by a mother who looks into a room where several children have been playing.

(*i*) *Not likely*!   This occurs as an emphatic answer to an unwelcome suggestion, such as: 'You wouldn't like to stay behind and wash the dishes, would you?' 'Not likely!'

(*j*) *H'm*!   This is often a comment of disapproval or disbelief: 'I was doing my best.' 'H'm!'

Part 7

1. (*a*) exclamatory, minor   (*b*) interrogative, major   (*c*) interrogative, major   (*d*) declarative, major   (*e*) exclamatory, major   (*f*) declarative, minor   (*g*) imperative, major   (*h*) interrogative, major   (*i*) imperative, major   (*j*) declarative, major.

2. (*a*) phrase   (*b*) clause   (*c*) phrase   (*d*) clause   (*e*) clause   (*f*) phrase   (*g*) clause   (*h*) phrase, phrase   (*i*) clause   (*j*) phrase

3.
Main clauses	*Subordinate clauses*
(*a*) The boat was full of holes	that I bought
(*b*) The fact was stressed	that she was beautiful
(*c*) Come in	when I ring the bell
(*d*) The man was wearing a brown coat	who escaped
	when I saw him
(*e*) He never failed an examination	although he rarely did any work

(*f*) Meet me	after you've finished work
(*g*) Do you think	he'll come
(*h*) That was	what he said
(*i*) Never say	that you'll do something if you have no intention of doing it
(*j*) Where did you put the book	I gave you

4. (*a*) adverb phrase of place   (*b*) noun phrase   (*c*) adverb phrase of manner   (*d*) adjective phrase   (*e*) predicate phrase   (*f*) noun phrase   (*g*) noun phrase   (*h*) adverb phrase of place; adverb phrase of place or manner   (*i*) predicate phrase   (*j*) adverb phrase of place

---

Part 8

---

1. (*a*) complement   (*b*) object   (*c*) subject; object   (*d*) complement   (*e*) predicate   (*f*) predicate   (*g*) subject   (*h*) predicate   (*i*) subject   (*j*) complement

2.

John	subject	proper noun
He	subject	pronoun
football	object	noun
His ambition	subject	noun phrase
History	object	proper noun
What	subject	pronoun
He	subject	pronoun
to be best at everything	object	non-finite phrase
Hard work	subject	noun phrase
success	subject	noun
great joy	object	noun phrase

3. (*a*) a bow and arrow (object, noun phrase)
   (*b*) me (object, pronoun); his friend (complement, noun phrase)
   (*c*) some cake (object, noun phrase)
   (*d*) a pilot (complement, noun phrase)
   (*e*) the bad news (object, noun phrase)
   (*f*) him (object, pronoun); the captain (complement, noun phrase)
   (*g*) to bet on the black mare (object, non-finite phrase)
   (*h*) ice-cream (object, noun phrase)
   (*i*) very gentle (complement, adjective phrase)
   (*j*) out (complement, adverb)

4. (*a*) him (indirect object)   (*b*) him (indirect object)   (*c*) her (indirect object)   (*d*) that (complement)   (*e*) home (complement)   (*f*) from the same town (complement)   (*g*) us

(indirect object) (*h*) irritable (complement) (*i*) me (indirect object) (*j*) him (indirect object)

5. should have been
thought   would last
was   was
had been building   were
hate   said
answered   have to admit   can be exciting

Part 9

1. (*b*) sang: John sang a *dirge*.
They sang *pop songs*.
She sang an *aria*.

   (*c*) refereed: Have you ever refereed *a game*?
She refereed *the hockey match*.
John refereed *the fight*.

   (*e*) put: John put *his money* in the bank.
He put *his foot* in the mud.
Put *it* wherever you like.

   (*g*) heard: I heard *your footsteps* on the path.
I heard *that he was dead*.
I heard *a loud bang* at 2 o'clock.

   (*j*) catch: I didn't want to catch *a cold*.
We'll catch *a later train*.
He won't catch *it* now.

2. (*a*) rang (pseudo-intrans.)   (*b*) rolled (intrans.)   (*c*) cooked (trans.)   (*d*) burn (intrans.); turn (trans.)   (*e*) broke (intrans.) (*f*) moved (trans.)   (*g*) dine (intrans.)   (*h*) sleep (intrans.) (*i*) take (trans.)   (*j*) is cooking (intrans.); smells (intrans.)

3. (*a*) John opened the door slowly.
1. The sentence with the agent is more explicit.
2. A sense of ambiguity and mystery.

   (*b*) Mary boiled the kettle.
1. The sentence with the agent is more explicit.
2. A sense of immediacy – the emphasis is on the kettle and not on a person.

   (*c*) I washed my shirt well.
1. The sentence with the agent is more explicit.
2. A sense of directness – the important fact is not who washed the shirt but how the shirt washed. This fact is more

clearly apparent in the non-agentive sentence.

(d) The shepherd put the sheep into the pen.
1. The sentence with the agent is more explicit.
2. A sense of ambiguity – the sheep could have acted out of habit or been put in by a dog or a shepherd.

(e) I have been cooking that chicken for two hours.
1. The sentence with the agent is more explicit.
2. The toughness of the chicken is emphasised by the non-agentive sentence.

(f) The thief stole the money.
1. The sentence with the agent is more explicit.
2. A sense of mystery.

(g) John started the car with a jerk.
1. The sentence with the agent is more explicit.
2. The first sentence does not put the blame on anyone.

(h) I tore my dress.
1. The sentence with the agent is more explicit.
2. The first sentence suggests that the tearing was an accident.

(i) John has changed his behaviour.
1. The sentence with the agent is more explicit.
2. The first sentence suggests that the change was unintentional.

(j) A mystery illness killed poor John.
1. Again, as in every other example, the sentence with the agent is more explicit because less capable of multiple interpretations.
2. The first sentence puts the emphasis mainly on John and not on the manner of his death.

4. (a) The old lady made her curtains shorter.
(b) John made the milk hot.
(c) The law has made this type of behaviour legal.
(d) He tampered with the evidence, making parts of it untrue.
(e) People seem to be made brutal by cruelty.
(f) He will have to be put into hospital.
(g) The mother gave food to the baby.
(h) Omo makes your whole wash brighter.
(i) This glass makes objects bigger.
(j) He caused the device to go off.

5. (a) We walked to the market.
(b) He filed the information.
(c) She wallpapered the room.
(d) They sandpapered the wood smooth.
(e) She fed the children.

Part 10

1. (*a*) flatter someone in order to get something from him
   (*b*) Don't draw attention to problems if the problems are not pressing.
   (*c*) a state of hostility that has not developed into a shooting war
   (*d*) one who moves around a lot, not staying long in any job
   (*e*) a person with limited ability in a wide range of skills
   (*f*) eccentric
   (*g*) extremely similar in appearance
   (*h*) make a wrong decision
   (*i*) tolerate
   (*j*) get into debt at the bank

2. (*a*) mouth: get one's information from a reliable source
   (*b*) hills: very old
   (*c*) hot: get into trouble or difficulties
   (*d*) good: be utterly altruistic, help someone without wanting anything in return
   (*e*) truth: change the facts to suit one's own interests
   (*f*) bone: have a reason to quarrel/find fault with someone
   (*g*) low: stay in the background
   (*h*) grass: seek support from the majority of the people
   (*i*) hatchet: agree to end hostilities
   (*j*) air: discuss misunderstandings openly so as to put an end to them

3. (*a*) go out celebrating/have an extremely lively celebration
   (*b*) limiting effects of bureaucracy
   (*c*) a day to remember forever/an exceptionally important day
   (*d*) deep in thought
   (*e*) a small lie/a lie that will not have serious repercussions. 'Little' or 'small' or 'insignificant' could substitute for 'white'
   (*f*) an important-looking but worthless possession
   (*g*) unofficial and illegal trade
   (*h*) be solvent/not owe the bank money
   (*i*) be in good health and spirits
   (*j*) be depressed

Part 11

1. *Consistency of vocabulary*, including the lexical set relating to baseball: 'superstar', 'outfielder', 'ball', 'American League', 'baseball', 'game', 'outfielders', 'warm-up', 'throws', 'plate', 'bottom', 'fifth inning', 'threw', 'ball', 'batboy', 'struck'.

Consistency of time reference: recent past implied by such verb forms as 'have charged', 'threw', 'struck', 'killed', 'occurred', 'completed', 'came' 'threw', 'struck'; and by the use of the time reference 'last night'.

Consistency of tone: simple sports journalism.

Links: use of pronouns 'he' and 'it' and possessive adjective 'their'; use of 'the incident' which sums up the information provided in the first paragraph.

2. John Smith loved only two people: himself and Mary Brown. Mary returned John's love but she worried about his character. She suspected that he might turn into a recluse, becoming increasingly alienated from society. If this happened, she feared that she might lose contact with her family and friends. Mary also worried about any children that she and John might have in case they grew up in isolation from society. For his part, John could not understand why Mary worried so much about people that he felt were not worth worrying about, and he told her to stop it.

3. (a) *Consistency of vocabulary*, including a lexical set relating to romance: 'feel', 'felt', 'hand in hand', 'we', 'sat', 'stray', 'May'.

    Consistency of time reference: starts in the non-past with 'wonder' and 'feel' and moves into the past with 'felt' and 'sat'.

    Consistency of tone: one lover's address to another and the reference to shared experiences.

    Links: use of pronouns 'I', 'you' and 'we'; use of conjunctions like 'as' and 'since'.

    Poetic linkage: rhythm with four strong stresses in lines 1–4 and three in line 5; rhyme scheme *a b a b a*; use of poetic licence with regard to word order, for instance the position of 'since' and 'better', and the choice of poetic forms such as 'morn' instead of 'morning'.

    (b) *Consistency of vocabulary*, including a lexical set relating to nature: 'grass', 'sweet', 'smell', 'sighing', 'sound', 'lights', 'shore'; and one relating to the senses – smell, sound, sight.

    Consistency of time reference: to the present and the recent past: 'have been', 'cannot tell', 'know'.

    Consistency of tone: descriptive, mysterious, evocative.

    Links: especially in the use of 'the', suggesting that the items referred to are known to the listener as well as the speaker.

    Poetic linkage: rhythm with a strong stress pattern of 3 4 4 3 5; rhyme scheme *a b a b a*; use of poetic licence with regard to word order in such a line as 'But when or how I cannot tell' instead of the more usual 'But I cannot tell when or how'; assonance, which is the repetition of the same vowel sounds. We find this in 'sweet' and 'keen' and again in 'sighing' and 'lights'.

(*c*) *Consistency of vocabulary*, including a lexical set relating to nature: 'nature', 'feet', 'meadow', 'dews', 'morning'.

Consistency of time reference: the use of modals 'will' and 'may' indicate that the reference to time is in the future.

Consistency of tone: one of resigned pessimism.

Links: use of conjunctions such as 'neither', 'nor', 'nor', 'and', 'if', 'or'.

Poetic linkage: rhythm with the pattern of strong stresses alternating between three and four 4 3 4 3 4 3; rhyme scheme *a b c b d b*; use of poetic licence with regard to word order and word choice. This is particularly apparent in the word order of line 2 and the use of 'no' rather than 'not' in line 6.

The most frequently used irregular nouns

Singular	Plural	Singular	Plural
child	children	louse	lice
datum	data	man	men
formula	formulae/formulas	mouse	mice
foot	feet	phenomenon	phenomena
fungus	fungi	tooth	teeth
goose	geese	woman	women
leaf	leaves		

Nouns which end with a consonant + y form their plural in 'ies':

beauty	beauties	caddy	caddies

Certain nouns ending in 'f' form their plurals in 'ves':

life	lives	thief	thieves
loaf	loaves	wife	wives
knife	knives	wolf	wolves
shelf	shelves		

Most nouns which end in 'ch', 'o', 's', 'sh', 'ss' or 'x' form their plurals with 'es':

catch	catches	bush	bushes
potato[1]	potatoes	pass	passes
gas	gases	box	boxes

The following nouns do not change their form in the plural:

buck	buck	grouse	grouse
deer	deer	sheep	sheep
fish	fish[2]		

NOTES:
[1] The two commonly used abbreviations 'photo' and 'piano' form their plurals by adding 's': 'photos', 'pianos'.
[2] Occasionally, especially in liturgically influenced English, we find the plural 'fishes'. The simplest rule for the student is to use 'fish' for both singular and plural.

The most frequently used irregular verbs

Base form	Past tense	Past participle	Non-past tense
be	was/were	been	am/are/is
beat	beat	beaten	beat/beats
become	became	become	become/becomes
begin	began	begun	begin/begins
bite	bit	bitten	bite/bites
bleed	bled	bled	bleed/bleeds
blow	blew	blown	blow/blows
broadcast[1]	broadcast	broadcast	broadcast/broadcasts
break	broke	broken	break/breaks
burn[2]	burned	burnt	burn/burns
buy	bought	bought	buy/buys
catch	caught	caught	catch/catches
choose	chose	chosen	choose/chooses
come	came	come	come/comes
creep	crept	crept	creep/creeps
dig	dug	dug	dig/digs
do	did	done	do/does
draw	drew	drawn	draw/draws
drink	drank	drunk	drink/drinks
drive	drove	driven	drive/drives

NOTES:

[1] A large number of verbs ending in 'd' and 't' do not show any change as between base form, past tense and past participle. The main verbs in this category are: **bet, burst, cast, cost, cut, hit, hurt, let, put, quit, set, shut, slit, thrust, upset, rid, shed, spread**.

[2] A number of verbs in English can have either 'ed' or 't' in both the past tense and the past participle. The commonest verbs in this group are: **burn, dream, leap, learn, smell, spell, spill**. There is a tendency in British English to use the 'ed' form for the past tense and the 't' form for the past participle.

Base form	Past tense	Past participle	Non-past tense
eat	ate	eaten	eat/eats
fall	fell	fallen	fall/falls
feed	fed	fed	feed/feeds
feel	felt	felt	feel/feels
fight	fought	fought	fight/fights
find	found	found	find/finds
fly	flew	flown	fly/flies
forbid	forbade	forbidden	forbid/forbids
forget	forgot	forgotten	forget/forgets
freeze	froze	frozen	freeze/freezes
get	got	got	get/gets
give	gave	given	give/gives
go	went	gone	go/goes
grow	grew	grown	grow/grows
have	had	had	have/has
hear	heard	heard	hear/hears
hide	hid	hidden	hide/hides
keep	kept	kept	keep/keeps
know	knew	known	know/knows
lay[3]	laid	laid	lay/lays
lead	led	led	lead/leads
leave	left	left	leave/leaves
lend	lent	lent	lend/lends
lie (i.e. stretch)	lay	lain	lie/lies
light	lit	lit	light/lights
lose	lost	lost	lose/loses
make	made	made	make/makes
mean	meant	meant	mean/means
meet	met	met	meet/meets
read[4]	read[5]	read[5]	read[4]/reads

NOTES:
[3] **pay** and **say** pattern in the same way as **lay**.
[4] This is pronounced to rhyme with 'reed'.
[5] This is pronounced to rhyme with 'red'.

Base form	Past tense	Past participle	Non-past tense
ride	rode	ridden	ride/rides
ring[6]	rang	rung	ring/rings
rise	rose	risen	rise/rises
run	ran	run	run/runs
see	saw	seen	see/sees
sell[7]	sold	sold	sell/sells
send	sent	sent	send/sends
shake[8]	shook	shaken	shake/shakes
shine	shone	shone	shine/shines
shoot	shot	shot	shoot/shoots
show	showed	shown	show/shows
sink	sank	sunk	sink/sinks
sit	sat	sat	sit/sits
shrink	shrank	shrunk	shrink/shrinks
sleep	slept	slept	sleep/sleeps
smell[9]	smelt	smelt	smell/smells
speak	spoke	spoken	speak/speaks
spend	spent	spent	spend/spends
spill	spilled	spilt	spill/spills
spit	spat	spat	spit/spits
stand[10]	stood	stood	stand/stands
steal	stole	stolen	steal/steals
stick	stuck	stuck	stick/sticks
stink	stank	stunk	stink/stinks
strike	struck	struck	strike/strikes
swear	swore	sworn	swear/swears
sweep	swept	swept	sweep/sweeps
swim	swam	swum	swim/swims

NOTES:

[6] **sing** patterns in the same way as **ring**.
[7] **tell** patterns in the same way as **sell**.
[8] **take** patterns in the same way as **shake**.
[9] **spell** patterns in the same way as **smell**.
[10] **understand** patterns in the same way as **stand**.

Base form	Past tense	Past participle	Non-past tense
teach	taught	taught	teach/teaches
tear[11]	torn	torn	tear/tears
think	thought	thought	think/thinks
throw	threw	thrown	throw/throws
wake	woke	woken	wake/wakes
wear[12]	wore	worn	wear/wears
win	won	won	win/wins
wind[13]	wound[14]	wound	wind/winds
write	wrote	written	write/writes

NOTES:

[11] This is pronounced to rhyme with 'bare'.
[12] This is pronounced to rhyme with 'bare'.
[13] This is pronounced to rhyme with 'mind'.
[14] This is pronounced to rhyme with 'round'.

Suggestions for further reading

This handbook provides the student with all the information and the terminology necessary to study the English language. Some students will, however, wish to further their knowledge and the following list will help them to do so.

CRYSTAL, DAVID: *Linguistics*, Penguin Books, Harmondsworth, 1973.

HEY, COLIN: *English Usage*, Longman/York Press, London 1983.

PALMER, F.: *Grammar*, Penguin Books, Harmondsworth, 1971.

SWAN, M.: *Practical English Usage*, Oxford University Press, London, 1980.

WEST, F.: *The Way of Language: An Introduction*, Harcourt Brace Jovanovich, New York, 1975.

Index

Further titles

ENGLISH USAGE
COLIN G. HEY

The correct and precise use of English is one of the keys to success in examinations. 'Compared with' or 'compared to'? 'Imply' or 'infer'? 'Principal' or 'principle'? Such questions may be traditional areas of doubt in daily conversation, but examiners do not take such a lenient view. The author deals with many of these tricky problems individually, but also shows that confidence in writing correct English comes with an understanding of how the English language has evolved, and of the logic behind grammatical structure, spelling and punctuation. The Handbook concludes with some samples of English prose which demonstrate the effectiveness and appeal of good English usage.

Colin G. Hey is a former Inspector of Schools in Birmingham and Chief Inspector of English with the Sudanese Ministry of Education.

A DICTIONARY OF LITERARY TERMS
MARTIN GRAY

Over one thousand literary terms are dealt with in this Handbook, with definitions, explanations and examples. Entries range from general topics (comedy, epic, metre, romanticism) to more specific terms (acrostic, enjambment, malapropism, onomatopoeia) and specialist technical language (catalexis, deconstruction, *haiku*, paeon). In other words, this single, concise volume should meet the needs of anyone searching for clarification of terms found in the study of literature.

Martin Gray is Lecturer in English at the University of Stirling.

AN INTRODUCTION TO LITERARY CRITICISM
RICHARD DUTTON

This is an introduction to a subject that has received increasing emphasis in the study of literature in recent years. As a means of identifying the underlying principles of the subject, the author examines the way in which successive eras and individual critics have applied different yardsticks by which to judge literary output. In this way the complexities of modern criticism are set in the perspective of its antecedents, and seen as only the most recent links in a chain of changing outlooks and methods of approach. The threads of this analysis are drawn together in the concluding chapter, which offers a blueprint for the practice of criticism.

Richard Dutton is Lecturer in English Literature at the University of Lancaster.

AN INTRODUCTORY GUIDE TO ENGLISH LITERATURE
MARTIN STEPHEN

This Handbook is the response to the demand for a book which could present, in a single volume, a basic core of information which can be generally regarded as essential for students of English literature. It has been specially tailored to meet the needs of students starting a course in English literature: it introduces the basic tools of the trade – genres, themes, literary terms – and offers guidance in the approach to study, essay writing, and practical criticism and appreciation. The author also gives a brief account of the history of English literature so that the study of set books can be seen in the wider landscape of the subject as a whole.

Martin Stephen is Second Master of Sedbergh School.

PREPARING FOR EXAMINATIONS IN ENGLISH LITERATURE
NEIL McEWAN

This Handbook is specifically designed for all students of English literature who are approaching those final months of revision before an examination. The purpose of the volume is to provide a sound background to the study of set books and topics, placing them within the context and perspective of their particular genres. The author also draws on his wide experience as a teacher of English both in England and abroad to give advice on approaches to study, essay writing, and examination techniques.

Neil McEwan is Lecturer in English at the University of Qatar.

READING THE SCREEN
An Introduction to Film Studies
JOHN IZOD

The world of cinema and television has become the focus of more and more literary work, and film studies is a fast-growing subject in schools and universities. The intention of this Handbook is to introduce the film viewer to the range of techniques available to the film maker for the transmission of a message, and to analyse the effects achieved by these techniques. This Handbook is geared in particular to students beginning a course in film studies – but it also has a great deal to offer any member of the film-going public who wishes to have a deeper understanding of the medium.

John Izod is Lecturer in Charge of Film and Media Studies at the University of Stirling.

York Notes: list of titles

CHINUA ACHEBE
A Man of the People
Arrow of God
Things Fall Apart

EDWARD ALBEE
Who's Afraid of Virginia Woolf?

ELECHI AMADI
The Concubine

ANONYMOUS
Beowulf
Everyman

JOHN ARDEN
Serjeant Musgrave's Dance

AYI KWEI ARMAH
The Beautyful Ones Are Not Yet Born

W. H. AUDEN
Selected Poems

JANE AUSTEN
Emma
Mansfield Park
Northanger Abbey
Persuasion
Pride and Prejudice
Sense and Sensibility

HONORÉ DE BALZAC
Le Père Goriot

SAMUEL BECKETT
Waiting for Godot

SAUL BELLOW
Henderson, The Rain King

ARNOLD BENNETT
Anna of the Five Towns

WILLIAM BLAKE
Songs of Innocence, Songs of Experience

ROBERT BOLT
A Man For All Seasons

ANNE BRONTË
The Tenant of Wildfell Hall

CHARLOTTE BRONTË
Jane Eyre

EMILY BRONTË
Wuthering Heights

ROBERT BROWNING
Men and Women

JOHN BUCHAN
The Thirty-Nine Steps

JOHN BUNYAN
The Pilgrim's Progress

BYRON
Selected Poems

ALBERT CAMUS
L'Etranger (The Outsider)

GEOFFREY CHAUCER
Prologue to the Canterbury Tales
The Franklin's Tale
The Knight's Tale
The Merchant's Tale
The Miller's Tale
The Nun's Priest's Tale
The Pardoner's Tale
The Wife of Bath's Tale
Troilus and Criseyde

ANTON CHEKHOV
The Cherry Orchard

SAMUEL TAYLOR COLERIDGE
Selected Poems

WILKIE COLLINS
The Moonstone
The Woman in White

SIR ARTHUR CONAN DOYLE
The Hound of the Baskervilles

WILLIAM CONGREVE
The Way of the World

JOSEPH CONRAD
Heart of Darkness
Lord Jim
Nostromo
The Secret Agent
Victory
Youth and *Typhoon*

STEPHEN CRANE
The Red Badge of Courage

BRUCE DAWE
Selected Poems

WALTER DE LA MARE
Selected Poems

DANIEL DEFOE
A Journal of the Plague Year
Moll Flanders
Robinson Crusoe

CHARLES DICKENS
A Tale of Two Cities
Bleak House
David Copperfield
Great Expectations
Hard Times
Little Dorrit
Nicholas Nickleby
Oliver Twist
Our Mutual Friend
The Pickwick Papers

EMILY DICKINSON
Selected Poems

JOHN DONNE
Selected Poems

THEODORE DREISER
Sister Carrie

GEORGE ELIOT
Adam Bede
Middlemarch
Silas Marner
The Mill on the Floss

T. S. ELIOT
Four Quartets
Murder in the Cathedral
Selected Poems
The Cocktail Party
The Waste Land

J. G. FARRELL
The Siege of Krishnapur

GEORGE FARQUHAR
The Beaux Stratagem

WILLIAM FAULKNER
Absalom, Absalom!
As I Lay Dying
Go Down, Moses
The Sound and the Fury

HENRY FIELDING
Joseph Andrews
Tom Jones

F. SCOTT FITZGERALD
Tender is the Night
The Great Gatsby

E. M. FORSTER
A Passage to India
Howards End

ATHOL FUGARD
Selected Plays

JOHN GALSWORTHY
Strife

MRS GASKELL
North and South

WILLIAM GOLDING
Lord of the Flies
The Inheritors
The Spire

OLIVER GOLDSMITH
She Stoops to Conquer
The Vicar of Wakefield

ROBERT GRAVES
Goodbye to All That

GRAHAM GREENE
Brighton Rock
The Heart of the Matter
The Power and the Glory

THOMAS HARDY
Far from the Madding Crowd
Jude the Obscure
Selected Poems
Tess of the D'Urbervilles
The Mayor of Casterbridge
The Return of the Native
The Trumpet Major
The Woodlanders
Under the Greenwood Tree

L. P. HARTLEY
The Go-Between
The Shrimp and the Anemone

NATHANIEL HAWTHORNE
The Scarlet Letter

SEAMUS HEANEY
Selected Poems

ERNEST HEMINGWAY
A Farewell to Arms
For Whom the Bell Tolls
The African Stories
The Old Man and the Sea

GEORGE HERBERT
Selected Poems

HERMANN HESSE
Steppenwolf

BARRY HINES
Kes

HOMER
The Iliad

ANTHONY HOPE
The Prisoner of Zenda

GERARD MANLEY HOPKINS
Selected Poems

WILLIAM DEAN HOWELLS
The Rise of Silas Lapham

RICHARD HUGHES
A High Wind in Jamaica

THOMAS HUGHES
Tom Brown's Schooldays

ALDOUS HUXLEY
Brave New World

HENRIK IBSEN
A Doll's House
Ghosts
Hedda Gabler

HENRY JAMES
Daisy Miller
The Europeans
The Portrait of a Lady
The Turn of the Screw
Washington Square

SAMUEL JOHNSON
Rasselas

BEN JONSON
The Alchemist
Volpone

JAMES JOYCE
A Portrait of the Artist as a Young Man
Dubliners

JOHN KEATS
Selected Poems

RUDYARD KIPLING
Kim

D. H. LAWRENCE
Sons and Lovers
The Rainbow
Women in Love

CAMARA LAYE
L'Enfant Noir

HARPER LEE
To Kill a Mocking-Bird

LAURIE LEE
Cider with Rosie

THOMAS MANN
Tonio Kröger

CHRISTOPHER MARLOWE
Doctor Faustus
Edward II

ANDREW MARVELL
Selected Poems

W. SOMERSET MAUGHAM
Of Human Bondage
Selected Short Stories

J. MEADE FALKNER
Moonfleet

HERMAN MELVILLE
Billy Budd
Moby Dick

THOMAS MIDDLETON
Women Beware Women

THOMAS MIDDLETON *and* WILLIAM ROWLEY
The Changeling

ARTHUR MILLER
Death of a Salesman
The Crucible

JOHN MILTON
Paradise Lost I & II
Paradise Lost IV & IX
Selected Poems

V. S. NAIPAUL
A House for Mr Biswas

SEAN O'CASEY
Juno and the Paycock
The Shadow of a Gunman

GABRIEL OKARA
The Voice

EUGENE O'NEILL
Mourning Becomes Electra

GEORGE ORWELL
Animal Farm
Nineteen Eighty-four

JOHN OSBORNE
Look Back in Anger

WILFRED OWEN
Selected Poems

ALAN PATON
Cry, The Beloved Country

THOMAS LOVE PEACOCK
Nightmare Abbey and *Crotchet Castle*

HAROLD PINTER
The Birthday Party
The Caretaker

PLATO
The Republic

ALEXANDER POPE
Selected Poems

THOMAS PYNCHON
The Crying of Lot 49

SIR WALTER SCOTT
Ivanhoe
Quentin Durward
The Heart of Midlothian
Waverley

PETER SHAFFER
The Royal Hunt of the Sun

WILLIAM SHAKESPEARE
A Midsummer Night's Dream
Antony and Cleopatra
As You Like It
Coriolanus
Cymbeline
Hamlet
Henry IV Part I
Henry IV Part II
Henry V
Julius Caesar
King Lear
Love's Labour's Lost
Macbeth
Measure for Measure
Much Ado About Nothing
Othello
Richard II
Richard III
Romeo and Juliet
Sonnets
The Merchant of Venice
The Taming of the Shrew
The Tempest
The Winter's Tale
Troilus and Cressida
Twelfth Night
The Two Gentlemen of Verona

GEORGE BERNARD SHAW
Androcles and the Lion
Arms and the Man
Caesar and Cleopatra
Candida
Major Barbara
Pygmalion
Saint Joan
The Devil's Disciple

MARY SHELLEY
Frankenstein

PERCY BYSSHE SHELLEY
Selected Poems

RICHARD BRINSLEY SHERIDAN
The School for Scandal
The Rivals

WOLE SOYINKA
The Lion and the Jewel
The Road
Three Short Plays

EDMUND SPENSER
The Faerie Queene (Book I)

JOHN STEINBECK
Of Mice and Men
The Grapes of Wrath
The Pearl

LAURENCE STERNE
A Sentimental Journey
Tristram Shandy

ROBERT LOUIS STEVENSON
Kidnapped
Treasure Island
Dr Jekyll and Mr Hyde

TOM STOPPARD
Professional Foul
Rosencrantz and Guildenstern are Dead

JONATHAN SWIFT
Gulliver's Travels

JOHN MILLINGTON SYNGE
The Playboy of the Western World

TENNYSON
Selected Poems

W. M. THACKERAY
Vanity Fair

DYLAN THOMAS
Under Milk Wood

EDWARD THOMAS.
Selected Poems

FLORA THOMPSON
Lark Rise to Candleford

J. R. R. TOLKIEN
The Hobbit
The Lord of the Rings

CYRIL TOURNEUR
The Revenger's Tragedy

ANTHONY TROLLOPE
Barchester Towers

MARK TWAIN
Huckleberry Finn
Tom Sawyer

VIRGIL
The Aeneid

VOLTAIRE
Candide

EVELYN WAUGH
Decline and Fall
A Handful of Dust

JOHN WEBSTER
The Duchess of Malfi
The White Devil

H. G. WELLS
The History of Mr Polly
The Invisible Man
The War of the Worlds

ARNOLD WESKER
Chips with Everything
Roots

PATRICK WHITE
Voss

OSCAR WILDE
The Importance of Being Earnest

TENNESSEE WILLIAMS
The Glass Menagerie

VIRGINIA WOOLF
To the Lighthouse

WILLIAM WORDSWORTH
Selected Poems

W. B. YEATS
Selected Poems

The author of this Handbook

LORETO TODD is a Senior Lecturer in English at the University of Leeds. Educated in Northern Ireland and Leeds she has degrees in English and Linguistics. Dr Todd has taught in England and in West Africa and has lectured in Australia, Papua New Guinea, the United States of America and the Caribbean. Her publications include ten books, among them *Pidgins and Creoles*, 1974; *Tortoise the Trickster*, 1979; *West African Pidgin Folktales*, 1979; *Variety in Contemporary English*, 1980; *Varieties of English around the World*, 1982; and *Modern Englishes*, 1984. She has written a number of articles on varieties of English, Pidgins and Creoles, folk traditions and literary stylistics. At present she is engaged in a study of the varieties and uses of spoken English. She is the author of four volumes in the York Notes Series and the forthcoming York Handbook *An Introduction to Linguistics*.